HEADWAY

WORKBOOK   **INTERMEDIATE**

John & Liz Soars

Oxford University Press

CW00410943

Oxford University Press
Walton Street, Oxford, OX2 6DP

Oxford New York Toronto
Delhi Bombay Calcutta Madras Karachi
Petaling Jaya Singapore Hong Kong Tokyo
Nairobi Dar es Salaam Cape Town
Melbourne Auckland

and associated companies in
Berlin Ibadan

OXFORD is a trade mark of Oxford University Press
ISBN 0 19 433556 9
© Oxford University Press 1986

First published 1986
Fifth impression 1988

All rights reserved. No part of this publication may be
reproduced, stored in a retrieval system or transmitted,
in any form or by any means, electronic, mechanical,
photocopying, recording, or otherwise, without the
prior permission of Oxford University Press.

This book is sold subject to the condition that it shall
not, by way of trade or otherwise, be lent, re-sold,
hired or otherwise circulated without the publisher's
prior consent in any form of binding or cover other than
that in which it is published and without a similar
condition including this condition being imposed on the
subsequent purchaser.

Filmset in Compugraphic Times and Univers
by VAP Group Ltd, Kidlington, Oxford.
Printed in Great Britain by St Edmundsbury Press Ltd
Bury St Edmunds, Suffolk

UNIT 1

The Present Simple (1)

1 Put the verb in brackets in the correct tense, *Present Simple* or *Present Continuous*.

a. Anne _____ (make) all her own clothes.

b. At the moment she _____ (make) a dress for herself.

c. What's that smell? Something _____ (burn) in the kitchen.

d. I _____ (work) overtime this month because I _____ (save up) to buy a car.

e. He _____ (smoke) thirty cigarettes a day, but at the moment he _____ (try) very hard to cut down.

f. The sun _____ (rise) in the east.

g. She usually _____ (learn) languages very fast, but she _____ (have) problems with Chinese.

2 Finish these sentences, and include an adverb of frequency. Be careful with the word order.

I don't write to my parents, but *I often phone them.* (phone)

a. He's a vegetarian, so he _____ _____. (meat)

b. I don't smoke cigarettes, but I _____ _____. (cigar after dinner)

c. We _____ Italy for our summer holidays because we have a villa there.

d. In winter we _____ go skiing in France, or we _____ at home. It depends.

e. We _____ fish because it is difficult to buy fresh.

Write some sentences about yourself, using an adverb of frequency.

I always have a cup of tea in the morning.

_____

_____

_____

_____

3 Contradict these sentences.

It doesn't rain in Britain.
Yes, it does.

a. Children start school when they're ten.

_____

b. Nurses don't wear uniforms.

_____

c. You aren't learning English.

_____

d. Linda McCartney comes from Scotland.

_____

e. It's snowing.

_____

f. Aspirin is good for a cough.

_____

g. You don't work hard.

_____

h. The best wine comes from Holland.

_____

4 Write an appropriate question for these answers.

A *Where do you come from?*
B I come from Manchester.

a. **A** _____ ?
   B I'm a teacher.

b. **A** _____ ?
   B Twenty-five hours a week. But of course I prepare lessons and mark exercises at home as well.

c. **A** _____ ?
   B At Manchester Grammar School.

d. **A** _____ ?
   B £10,000 a year.

e. **A** _____ abroad ?
   B Once or twice a year, usually to Germany.

f. **A** _____ evenings ?
   B No, not a lot. I'm usually too tired, but I sometimes go to the cinema.

g. **A** _____
   B I like all sorts, but expecially westerns and comedies.

h. **A** _____
   B I'm going to the pub to meet some friends. Would you like to come?

5 Write about what these people do at work and what they're doing now. Look at the example carefully.

At work   Now

Sandra is an air hostess. She works for Pan Am. She flies all over the world and works long hours. She serves meals and looks after the passengers. She stays in hotels a lot. She wears a uniform. At the moment she's playing tennis with a friend. She's wearing a tennis skirt. Some people are watching them.

At work   Now

a. Ed is a policeman in New York. _____

_____

_____

_____

_____

_____

_____

At work   Now

b. Amy and Peter own a restaurant. _____

_____

_____
_____
_____

At work   Now

c. Noriko is a doctor in Tokyo. _____

_____
_____
_____
_____

6 High Street shops

Why do you go to these places?
What do they sell or do?

a heel bar
You go to a heel bar if your shoes need repairing.

a baker
A baker sells bread, rolls, and cakes.

a. a newsagent

_____

b. a DIY shop

_____

c. an off-licence

_____

d. a building society

_____

e. a garden centre

_____

f. a book shop

_____

g. a library

_____

h. an estate agent

_____

i. a jeweller

_____

j. a hardware shop

_____

k. a chemist

_____

l. a freezer centre

_____

m. a sports shop

_____

n. a florist

_____

o. a travel agent

_____

7 Pronunciation

's' at the end of a word has three different
pronunciations.

/z/ sells   /s/ works   /ɪz/ washes

Look at pages 1 and 2 of the Student's Book. Put the
verbs in the profile that are in the third person singular
on the right lines below.

/z/   *lives* _____

/s/   _____

/ɪz/ _____

Can you add to the list?

8 Look at 'A life in the day of' in the Student's Book on
page 4. Write about a typical day in your life. Say
what you do usually/always/sometimes. Include the
following.

– Routine: get up, exercise, evenings
– Work: when, where, how long
– Food and meals
– Family

UNIT 2

The Present Simple (2)

1 You have a guest, Henry, staying at your house, and you want to look after him. Write an appropriate question for each situation.

What would you like to . . . ?
Would you like something . . . ?
Would you like a . . . ?

Write an appropriate answer.

Yes, I'd love to.
I'd like a . . ., please.
Yes, I'd like a . . ., please.
Yes, I would.

He's thirsty.
You *Would you like something to drink?*
Henry *Yes, I'd like a cup of tea, please.*

a. He's hungry.

You _____

_____

Henry _____

_____

b. He likes tennis, and it's a nice day.

You _____

_____

Henry _____

_____

c. He's got a headache.

You _____

_____

Henry _____

_____

d. It's cold, and he hasn't got any warm clothes.

You _____

_____

Henry _____

_____

e. He's interested in historic buildings.

You _____

_____

Henry _____

_____

f. You'd like a game of cards.

You _____

_____

Henry _____

_____

g. There's a good film on television.

You _____

_____

Henry _____

_____

2 Match a question in column **A** with an answer in column **B**.

A
a ☐ Would you like ice in your whisky?
b ☐ Do you like Italian food?
c ☐ Do you like dancing?
d ☐ What do you like doing on holiday?
e ☐ Would you like an Italian meal tonight?
f ☐ Would you like to dance?

B

1 Yes, especially modern.
2 As little as possible.
3 Thank you, but I'm too tired at the moment.
4 Yes. Do you know a good restaurant?
5 No thanks. Just on its own.
6 Yes, but I think it's fattening.

3 Present Simple or Present Continuous

Some of these sentences are in the wrong tense.
Correct them on the line below if necessary.

e.g. It rains at the moment. ✗
   It's raining. ✓

   I get up at seven in the morning. ✓
   _____

a. I'm liking black coffee.
   _____

b. He's speaking three languages.
   _____

c. I think Mexico's a beautiful country.
   _____

d. Restaurants are staying open late in Spain.
   _____

e. We usually eat at one o'clock.
   _____

f. He's having a flat near the centre.
   _____

g. What are you thinking of Shakespeare?
   _____

h. I'm so dirty I need a bath right now.
   _____

i. Peter's in the kitchen. He cooks breakfast.
   _____

j. What are you thinking about?
   _____

4 Inviting people out

Write similar dialogues of invitation.

A I'm going to the cinema tonight. Would you like to come with me?
B What are you going to see?
A *The Killing Fields.*
B What sort of film is it?
A I think it's a war film.
B Yes, I'd love to come. Where's it on?

A The Classic in Tottenham Court Road.
B What time does it start?
A The last show is at 8.00.
B I'll meet you outside at 7.30. How's that?
A Right. I'll see you then.

THE KILLING FIELDS
NOW SHOWING *CLASSIC* TOTTENHAM COURT ROAD 636 6148
2.10, 5.00, 8.00. Late shows Fri and Sat 11.15pm

Prince Edward Theatre
Tim Rice and Andrew Lloyd Webber's

EVITA
The Giant of Musicals
Evenings 8.00
Matinees Thur and Sat at 3.00

蓮花酒家 *Lotus Flower*
CHINESE RESTAURANT

Special vegetarian dishes

Open from 6.00 till midnight
34 Green Lane, Putney

5

5 Describing

Look at the sentences. Are they describing . . .
a. a film?
b. a football match?
c. a meal?

Are they positive (saying something nice), or negative (saying something not nice)?
First decide what they are describing, then put a. b. or c. in the first box, and + or − sign in the second box.

1 ☐ ☐ Robinson scored a superb goal from thirty yards.
2 ☐ ☐ The first course was delicious.
3 ☐ ☐ Jane Holgar's performance as the flower seller was rather weak.
4 ☐ ☐ The speciality of the day was good value.
5 ☐ ☐ In the second half both teams played badly.
6 ☐ ☐ The shots of the countryside were beautiful.
7 ☐ ☐ The chop was too fatty and the salad too oily.
8 ☐ ☐ The referee made some poor decisions.
9 ☐ ☐ If you like suspense, I would recommend it.
10 ☐ ☐ The recipe is easy and the ingredients are cheap.

6 Vocabulary of professions

In this list of words, there are four professions and four words associated with each profession. Put the words in the correct column. Use your dictionary to check the meaning and the pronunciation.

a chef	an article	the Stock Market
a bandage	to interview	a national daily paper
a headline	an X-ray	to give an injection
to roast	a spoon	an oven
a factory	a nurse	a thermometer
an editor	to make a profit	a businessman
a briefcase	a frying-pan	

a chef	

7 Hear   listen to   see   look at   watch

Put in one of these verbs in the right form. Remember that **hear** and **see** need **can** or **can't**.

a. I have a lovely view from my room. I _____ _____ the whole city.

b. **A**: What's Peter doing?
   B: He _____ music in his bedroom.

c. In winter I like _____ the photographs of my summer holiday.

d. In the evening I usually _____ the news on television.

e. I find it difficult to sleep because I _____ the traffic all night.

f. Can you speak louder? You're speaking so quietly that I _____ you.

g. _____ that strange man over there! What's he doing?

h. Please _____ what I'm saying. It's very important.

i. **A**: Where's Maria?
   B: Over there. She _____ the picture on the wall.

j. Oh dear! Where are my glasses? I _____ anything without them.

8 Look at the Fact File of Willi Hoffmann on page 7 of the Student's Book.

Write a similar fact file on a well-known international person, from the world of politics, sport or show-business.
Include information about his/her background, family life, work habits and beliefs.

_____
_____
_____
_____
_____
_____
_____
_____

UNIT 3

Past Simple and Past Continuous

1 Put the verb in brackets in the correct tense, *Past Simple* or *Past Continuous*.

  a. Last year I _____ (go) to Greece for my holidays.

  b. I _____ (decide) to fly because it is much quicker than going overland.

  c. On the morning I left London, it _____ (rain), but when I _____ (step) off the plane in Greece, it was a beautiful day. The sun _____ (shine), and a cool wind _____ (blow) from the sea.

  d. I _____ (take) a taxi to my hotel. As I _____ (sign) the register, someone _____ (tap) me on the shoulder. I _____ (turn) round. It was a friend I hadn't seen for ten years. He _____ (stay) at the same hotel.

  e. That evening we _____ (go) for a walk. The town was still very busy. Street traders _____ (sell) souvenirs, and the foreign tourists _____ (try) to bring down the price with the aid of a Greek phrase book. We _____ (listen) to their chatter for a while, then returned to our hotel.

2 Look at the story about Mary Padley on page 16 of the Student's Book. Contradict and correct these sentences about her.

Mary doesn't smoke.

Yes she does. She smokes cigarettes and cigars.

  a. She recently celebrated her wedding anniversary.

  _____

  b. She didn't have a party.

  _____

  c. She was born in Wales.

  _____

  d. She never left Ireland.

  _____

  e. She was working as a cook when she met her husband.

  _____

3 Write an appropriate question for these answers.

A *How old were you when you started school?*
B I was six years old.

  a. **A** _____
    B I went to two schools.

  b. **A** _____
    B The first was a junior school, the second was a grammar school.

  c. **A** _____
    B No, I didn't. I really hated them. I was very unhappy at school.

  d. **A** _____
    B I took 'O' levels when I was 15, and 'A' levels when I was 17.

  e. **A** _____
    B Yes, I did. I went to Oxford University.

  f. **A** _____
    B Modern languages – French and German.

  g. **A** _____
    B I was there for four years.

7

h. **A** _____

   B I left in 1978.

Write a short paragraph giving your academic background. Say what schools you went to and what exams you passed.

_____

_____

_____

_____

_____

_____

_____

_____

_____

_____

4 Prepositions of time

Put in the correct prepositions, **in, at,** or **on**.

a. I get up early _____ the morning and go to bed late

   _____ night.

b. I'm so bored. There's nothing to do _____ week-ends.

c. He went swimming _____ Sunday morning, and

   _____ the evening he played squash.

d. I love going for walks _____ summer. It's still light

   _____ nine o'clock.

e. I take my annual holiday _____ June, but I have a

   few days off _____ Christmas.

f. He usually starts work _____ 9.30, but _____

   Fridays he starts _____ 8.30.

g. I was born _____ 1951.

h. I was born _____ 18 January, 1954.

i. People exchange presents _____ Christmas Day.

j. This house was built _____ the nineteenth century.

What time expressions are used with these prepositions? Fill in these lists and add more if you can.

in *the morning*	at *night*	on *Sunday morning*
_____	_____	_____
_____	_____	_____
_____	_____	_____
_____	_____	_____
_____	_____	_____

5 Pronunciation

There are three different pronunciations of the **-ed** in regular past tenses.

/d/ travelled   /t/ watched   /ɪd/ wanted

Put these past tenses on the right lines below according to the pronunciation of **-ed.**

hoped	rescued	climbed	decided
arrived	moved	used	planted
washed	stopped	walked	helped
posted	crashed	ended	stayed

/d/ _____

_____

/t/ *hoped*

_____

/ɪd/ _____

_____

6 Vocabulary: Silent letters

All these words contain letters that are not pronounced. Cross out the unpronounced letters.

Example

cas~~t~~le   ha~~l~~f   ~~h~~our

climb	comb	Christmas	daughter
theatre	autumn	listen	calm
farm	February	cupboard	psychology
turn	sign	sandwich	handkerchief
Wednesday	honest	centre	
know	wrap	iron	
talk	write	island	

7 **Vocabulary**: Words often confused
Put the correct word into the gap.

birth   birthday   born

a. What is your place of _____?

b. When is your _____?

c. I was _____ in Africa.

d. She gave _____ to a healthy boy.

e. Where were you _____?

die   died   dead   death

f. Shakespeare _____ in 1616.

g. Her father's _____ came as a great surprise.
He was only 45.

h. Those flowers are _____. Throw them away.

i. Every winter many birds _____ in cold
weather.

j. **A** Is Henry Jones still alive?

   B I'm sure he's _____. Didn't he _____

   _____ about three years ago?

married   get married   got married   marry

k. **A** Are you _____?
   B No, I'm single.

l. **A** Whatever happened to Anne?

   B She _____ a man she
   met on holiday.

m. I'm never going to _____
again. I prefer being on my own.

n. How many times have you been _____

   _____?

o. Darling, I love you. Will you _____

   _____ me?

p. We had a lovely wedding. We _____

   _____ in a small country church, and had
the reception in the local hotel.

q. Did you hear? James and Henrietta _____

   _____ last week.

8 John and his family have just come back from holiday.
They are going through Customs, and the Customs
Officer wants to know the details of their holiday. But
John contradicts himself. Can you find his mistakes?

John Well, we left England on the 4th, and it's now
the 29th, so we have been away just over a fortnight.
We stayed in the country. We didn't go to any big
towns. We drove straight to a farmhouse that we were
renting, without stopping.

We didn't have very good weather, unfortunately.
While we were there we bought some very nice
pottery for my father, but apart from that we didn't
really buy anything. We went swimming every day,
but didn't travel around at all.

We left the house a few days ago. We probably
won't see it again, because we're going to sell it this
winter and buy somewhere in Spain. The hotel on the
way back was nicer than the one on the journey there,
and the children liked Paris very much.

Customs Officer Have you got anything to declare?

John We didn't buy any presents for anyone, but we
bought some wine from a farm about sixty kilometres
from our farmhouse. That's all.

Customs Officer Could I look through your car,
please?

Write about your last holiday. If you like, you can
make some mistakes, too. Show your story to another
student, and see if he or she can find the mistakes.

_____

_____

_____

_____

_____

_____

_____

_____

_____

_____

_____

_____

_____

_____

UNIT 4

Asking People to Do Things

1 Social situations

Write two-line dialogues for the following situations.

You are in a room, feeling very hot. What do you say to the person sitting near the window?

You *Excuse me! Could you open the window please?*
B *Yes, of course.* _____

a. You are in a restaurant. You have finished your meal and want to pay. What do you ask the waiter?

You _____

Waiter _____

b. You are a car mechanic. A friend is in trouble because his car won't start. What do you say?

You _____

Friend _____

c. A friend needs to get to the airport as quickly as possible. You have a car.

You _____

Friend _____

d. You have a cigarette but no matches. You see someone smoking. What do you ask?

You _____

B _____

e. You want to make a phone call, but you only have a one-pound coin. What do you ask a passer-by in the street?

You _____

Passer-by _____

f. Some friends want to go out tonight, but need someone to look after their children. You are free. What do you say?

You _____

Friends _____

g. Your next-door neighbours' television is very loud, and you can't sleep. You knock on their door. What do you say?

You _____

Neighbours _____

2

On this page there are two dialogues, but they are mixed up. Sort them out, and put them in the right order.

In Dialogue 1, Mr Monroe and Mrs Walsh are talking in an office.
In Dialogue 2, Ned is talking to a friend of his, Jamie, at home.

The first line of each dialogue has been given to you.

a. I'll certainly help if I can.

b. Here you are.

c. Jamie, could you give me a hand?

d. OK. I'm coming.

e. Yes, Mrs Walsh. What is it?

f. Thank you very much. That's very kind.

g. Well, I have a bit of a problem. I was wondering if you could help me.

h. What do you want? I'm busy.

i. Thanks.

j. I need to go to the airport after work. Do you think you could give me a lift?

k. Excuse me, Mr Monroe. Have you got a minute?

l. I'm trying to fix this door and I need something.

m. Of course. I drive past it on my way home.

n. Can you see that screwdriver over there? Can you give it to me?

Dialogue 1		Dialogue 2	
Mrs Walsh	*(k)*	Ned	*(c)*
Mr Monroe	_____	Jamie	_____
Mrs Walsh	_____	Ned	_____
Mr Monroe	_____	Jamie	_____
Mrs Walsh	_____	Ned	_____
Mr Monroe	_____	Jamie	_____
Mrs Walsh	_____	Ned	_____

In both dialogues, one person is asking the other to do something. Compare the differences.

I was wondering if you could help me?
Could you give me a hand?

3 What sort of thing do you ask these people to do for you?

a hairdresser *Could you wash and cut my hair, please?/Could you just trim it for me?*

a. a taxi driver

_____

_____

b. a plumber

_____

_____

c. an electrician

_____

_____

d. a dry cleaner

_____

_____

e. room service in a hotel

_____

_____

4 **Vocabulary**
bring   take   fetch

Put one of these verbs in the appropriate form in each gap.

a. Could you _____ my library books back for me? They're due back today.

b. Look! I _____ you a present. This is for you.

c. The postman has just been. Could you _____ _____ the letters, please?

d. When travelling abroad, you should _____ your passport.

e. Teacher to students: When you come to class, could you please remember to _____ your course book and dictionary?

f. **A:** Have you seen my blue suit anywhere?

   B: I _____ it to the dry cleaners for you.

g. I've forgotten my car keys. They're on the shelf in the kitchen. Could you _____ them for me?

h. Peter, could you _____ me to the station on your way to work?

i. (On the phone)
   A Hello, Dad? I'm at the station. Could you do me a favour? Could you _____ me?
   B Why can't you get the bus?
   A There isn't one for another hour.

j. Shop assistant to customer: Don't worry. If you don't like the hat, _____ it back to the shop and I'll change it for you.

5 **Vocabulary**

Think of a country for each letter of the alphabet. Write the adjective too. Some aren't easy! One or two are perhaps impossible. Compare your answers with a partner.

A	*Australia*	E	_____
	Australiàn		_____
B	_____	F	_____
	_____		_____
C	_____	G	_____
	_____		_____
D	_____	H	_____
	_____		_____

11

I _____   R _____

_____   _____

J _____   S _____

_____   _____

K _____   T _____

_____   _____

L _____   U _____

_____   _____

M _____   V _____

_____   _____

N _____   W _____

_____   _____

O _____   X _____

_____   _____

P _____   Y _____

_____   _____

Q _____   Z _____

_____   _____

6 Here is part of the story about Mrs Gibbs. There are nine gaps. Put one of the following words into each gap.

for   during   ago   while

Mrs Gibb's husband died about fifteen years

(a) _____ and to help her get over his death she decided to go abroad. She went to the Far East

(b) _____ six months, found she liked travelling and so planned to travel more on her own.

(c) _____ the winter of 1976 she bought and equipped a small camping van. Next summer she set

off for Australia, where she stayed (d) _____ two years. She went to America for the first time five

years (e) _____, and is going back this year. She plans to travel round Canada and America

(f) _____ the next eighteen months. She says she has never been frightened, but once, seven years

(g) _____ someone came into her van and

stole some papers. It happened (h) _____ she was driving through Zimbabwe. She heard a noise

(i) _____ the night, but paid no attention.

7 Write a short paragraph. What countries would you like to visit? Why? How long would you like to stay there?

_____

_____

_____

_____

_____

_____

_____

_____

_____

_____

_____

_____

_____

_____

_____

_____

_____

_____

_____

_____

_____

_____

UNIT 5

Will and Going To

1 Complete these sentences, using **will** or **going to**.
a. **A** Poor Sue went to hospital yesterday.

   B I'm sorry to hear that. I _____ some flowers.
b. **A** This room's very cold.

   B You're right. I _____ the heater.
c. **A** Are you still going out with Alice?

   B Oh yes. We _____ get married next year.
d. **A** Oh dear. I can't do this homework.

   B Don't worry. I _____ you.
e. **A** Did you remember to book seats for the theatre?

   B No, I forgot. I _____ now.
f. **A** It's John's birthday tomorrow.

   B Is it? I can't afford a present but I _____

   _____ a card.
g. **A** How old are you?

   B I'm 64. I _____ retire next year.
h. **A** Why are you buying so much food?

   B Because I _____ cook for ten people.
i. **A** Jack is very angry with you.

   B Is he? I didn't realize. I _____ ring him and apologize.
j. **A** Why are you leaving so early?
   B Because the teacher gave us a lot of homework

   and I _____ very carefully.

2 Complete the second line of these dialogues.

   A I've got a terrible headache.
   B I'll *get you an aspirin.*

a. **A** I haven't got any money at all.

   B I'll _____.

b. **A** John and Ann have just had a baby.

   B Have they? I'll _____.
c. **A** What's Jeremy's phone number?

   B Just a minute. I'll _____.
d. **A** I've lost my dog.

   B Don't worry. I'll _____.
e. **A** What's the weather forecast for today?

   B I don't know. I'll _____.

3 Answer the questions about your next holiday.

   A I'm going on holiday next week.
   B Where to?

   A _____
   B That sounds lovely. Where are you going to stay?

   A _____
   B And what are you going to do? Relax, or see the sights, or both?

   A _____

   _____
   B How are you getting there?

   A _____
   B And how long are you away for?

   A _____
   B Lucky you. Have a good time.
   A I'll send you a postcard.

4 Think of an answer to these questions. Give a reason to support what you say.

   A What's the weather going to be like this afternoon?
   B *I think it's going to rain. That's what the forecast said.*

13

a. **A** Do you think you'll be happy in your new house?

B _____

_____

b. **A** What do you think the new government will do about unemployment?

B _____

_____

_____

_____

_____

c. **A** What will your mother say when she sees your haircut?

B _____

_____

_____

d. **A** When you get out of prison, what's the first thing you're going to do?

B _____

_____

e. **A** I wonder what'll happen to that man who won half a million pounds on the football pools.

B _____

_____

5 Put one of the following words into each gap.
**some   someone   something   somewhere
any   anyone   anything**

a. **A** Did you buy _____ at the shops?

B No, I didn't have _____ money.

b. **A** Can I have _____ to eat, Mum? I'm starving.

B Look in the fridge. I think there's _____ cheese.

A There isn't _____ in the fridge. It's completely empty.

c. **A** Did you meet _____ interesting at the party?

B Yes, I met _____, _____ you know. Carlos, from Spain.

d. **A** I bought _____ meat and _____ grapes.

B Did you buy _____ cooking oil?

A I couldn't. They didn't have _____.

e. **A** Have you got _____ scissors?

B Yes. They are _____ in the kitchen, but I'm not sure exactly where.

6 **Prefixes and suffixes**

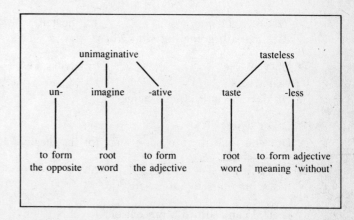

Prefixes	Meaning	Example
un-	opposite	**uncommon**
in-	opposite	**incorrect**
over-	too much	**oversleep**

Suffixes	Meaning	Example
-less	without	**defenceless**
-ive		**constructive**
-able	adjective	**fashionable**
-ible		**horrible**
-ous		**humorous**
-ly	adverb	**slowly**

Read the text on page 26 of the Students' Book and underline the words with these prefixes and suffixes.

The words in brackets can be used to form words that fit into the following sentences.

Artists are *creative* people. (create)

a. John is _____ hardworking. (extreme)

b. I didn't like the food. I found it most _____. (pleasant)

c. He was sacked from his job because he was _____. (efficient)

d. She was arrested because she was driving _____. (care)

e. It was very _____ of him not to help you. (kind)

f. My wife likes the colour blue, but I find it _____. (attract)

g. He's a lucky man. He's been _____ married for eight years. (happy)

h. I bought a new car because the old one was so _____. (rely)

i. The dancer was superb. She gave a _____ performance. (fault)

j. The passengers were frightened when the pilot flew _____ close to a building. (danger)

7 **Food vocabulary**

a. What is the difference between these different ways of cooking food?
to grill   to roast   to fry   to bake   to boil
What parts of the cooker are used?

b. What food can be eaten
scrambled   boiled   fried   poached ?

c. What's the difference between
to cut   to chop   to peel ?

d. What's the opposite of . . .
dry wine   a **well-done** steak?
tough meat?   a **clear** soup?
cooked fish?   a **heavy** meal?
fresh bread?   **undercooked** vegetables?

8 Describe a meal that is particularly memorable. Where were you? Who were you with? What did you have? Why was it special?

_____

_____

_____

_____

_____

_____

Revision

1 Here is a letter from Anna to a friend of hers. There are twenty gaps. Some gaps have a verb in brackets. Put the verb in the correct tense.

   Yesterday I *went* (go) to the park.

When there is no verb in brackets, put in ONE suitable word — perhaps a preposition, an adverb, a modal verb, etc.

   I came *to* London to learn English.

Dear Miguel,
   I thought you would like to know some of my news.

I (a) _____ (arrive) in London two weeks

(b) _____ and I (c) _____

(stay) with a family in Paddington called the Boltons.

They're very nice. Mrs Bolton (d) _____

(work) in a bank, but at the moment Mr Bolton

(e) _____ (not have) a job. He

(f) _____ (do) a course in business management which starts next month.

I (g) _____ (have) a good time in London,

(h) _____ the work is boring. I (i)

_____ like to change and find a job that's

a little more (j) _____. I think I (k) _____ start looking soon.

I (l) _____ (travel) on the underground the

other day (m) _____ I met Pedro. Do you

remember him? When we last (n) _____

(see) him, he (o) _____ (work) for his

15

father's company. Now he (p) _____
(learn) English at a private school here. We (q)

_____ (see) an art exhibition together this
afternoon. I'm really looking forward to it.

I like London very much, but I (r) _____

(think) it's very expensive. (s) _____ you
do me a favour? I need some more money. Of course I

(t) _____ pay you back when I see you.

Take care.

Lots of love,

Anna

2 Write a letter like Anna's to a friend of yours. Include
some
recent news (past tenses)
future plans (future tenses)
information about your present life (present tenses).

First think of somewhere you went recently, or
someone you met, and something you're going to do
soon.

Dear _____

_____

_____

_____

_____

_____

_____

_____

_____

_____

_____

_____

_____

_____

3 Write what you would say in the following situations.

a. You are at a friend's house. You have just spilt a
cup of coffee on the carpet.

_____

_____

b. There's a good film on at the cinema. Invite a
friend to see it with you.

_____

c. You are in a town you don't know. You want to
find a post office. What do you ask someone in the
street?

_____

_____

d. You're in a town you don't know. Someone asks
you the way to the post office.

_____

e. You're in a shop. You buy a magazine which costs
70p, and give the assistant a £5 note. He gives you
30p change.

_____

_____

4 Complete these sentences in a suitable way.

a. I didn't have any money because _____

_____.

b. I decided to get a job, so I _____

_____.

c. At first I was quite optimistic, but _____

_____.

d. Then, while I _____

_____, I met a man who offered to help.

e. He knew someone who _____

_____.

f. I went for the interview and _____

_____.

g. I took the job. The pay is good, although _____

_____.

h. I'd like to leave the job, but _____

_____.

UNIT 6

Describing People and Places

1 Write an appropriate question for these situations.

a. You are going to meet a friend of your sister at the airport. You've never met her before. What do you ask your sister?

_____

_____

b. A friend has just been to visit Alice in hospital. What do you ask?

_____

c. 'There was a new student in our class today. She's Japanese,' says a friend of yours. What question do you ask?

_____

d. You have invited some friends to come to your house for a meal. You want to make sure that you don't give them food they don't like. What do you ask them?

_____

e. You were in a bank when it was robbed by three men. You saw the men. What question do the police ask you?

_____

f. A friend is reading a letter from his girlfriend. You want to know if she is well. What do you ask?

_____

g. A friend has just come back from two weeks in the Bahamas. You know nothing about these islands. What do you ask?

_____

_____

2 Answer these questions.

a. What sort of things do you like doing?

_____

_____

b. How are your parents?

_____

c. Who do you look like in your family?

_____

d. What are you like as a person?

_____

_____

e. What's your school like?

_____

f. What does your teacher look like?

_____

3 Use the suggestions in the right-hand column and your own ideas to complete this dialogue. Jeremy is talking to Paul, who's looking for somewhere to live.

Jeremy You don't look very cheerful. What's the matter?

Paul _____ problem

_____ somewhere/anywhere

_____ to live

_____

Jeremy Are you looking for a flat?
Paul _____
Jeremy Well, a friend of mine has got a big house with a flat in it. Are you interested?
Paul Very. What's it like?

Jeremy _____ West London

_____ park

_____ cinema

_____ noisy

_____ bedroom

_____ living-room

_____ kitchen

_____ bathroom

_____ garden

Paul It sounds absolutely great! And you say this friend of yours lives in the same house. What's he like?
Jeremy _____ Bill

_____ Canadian

_____ Montreal

_____ wife

_____ children

_____ doctor

_____ local hospital

_____ very nice

_____ likes cinema and rugby

_____

_____ hates people who smoke

_____

Paul That's all right. I've just given up. Listen, this really sounds great. When can I see the flat?
Jeremy I'm going over there tonight, actually. Why don't you come with me?

Paul _____

_____

Jeremy Yes, I'm sure he'll be in tomorrow. I'll tell you how to get there.

_____

_____

_____

_____

He lives at number 34, Princes Road.
Paul That's wonderful. I'll go tomorrow. Thanks a lot.

4 **Vocabulary:** Opposites (Antonyms)

What's the opposite of . . .?
an old house   _a new house_
an old man   _a young man_

a. dark hair

_____

b. a dark room

_____

c. a single person

_____

d. a single ticket

_____

e. a sweet apple

_____

f. sweet wine

_____

g. a strong man

_____

h. strong beer

_____

i. rich food

_____

j. a rich person

_____

k. a hard exam

_____

l. a hard chair

_____

m. a hot drink

_____

n. a hot curry

_____

5 Vocabulary: Synonyms

Think of a similar word for . . .

a pretty girl   *an attractive girl*
a handsome man   *a good-looking man*

a. a rich man

_____

b. an unhappy situation

_____

c. my usual routine

_____

d. a funny story

_____

e. a well-dressed person

_____

f. a soft voice

_____

g. an untidy room

_____

h. a badly-behaved child

_____

6 Complete these sentences. You will need to include a comparative form, and also verbs, articles, etc.

a. France is _____ England in

area, but England _____
population.

b. My new job is very interesting. I have to work

_____ in my old job, and the

hours _____, but the salary

_____, so I don't mind. Also

there are _____ promotion.

c. I sold my Mercedes and bought a Mini because

_____

_____

_____

7 Compare the following briefly.

a. Travelling by train and travelling by car.

_____

_____

_____

_____

_____

b. Package holidays and holidays you organize for yourself.

_____

_____

_____

_____

c. The difference between your life now and your life five years ago.

_____

_____

_____

_____

_____

d. The English language and your own.

_____

_____

_____

_____

_____

_____

UNIT 7

Present Perfect Simple

1 Put the verb in brackets in the correct tense, Present Perfect Simple or Past Simple.

a. Carlos _____ (come) to London before

Christmas. When he _____ (arrive), he

_____ (go) to stay with some friends.
He _____ (be) in London for several
months, and he's going to stay until the autumn.

b. **A** I'm looking for Susan. _____ you

_____ (see) her?

B I _____ (see) her yesterday, but not

today. _____ you _____
(look) in the coffee bar?

A Yes. I _____ (go) there before I
_____ (ask) you.

c. **A** John, you know I _____ (borrow)

your bicycle last night. Well, I'm afraid I

_____ (lose) it.

B That's awful! Where _____ you

_____ (go)? What time _____
_____ it _____ (happen)?

A Well, I _____ (leave) your house at

8.00, went home and _____ (chain)
it outside my house. Someone must have taken it

during the night. I _____ (phone)

the police, and they're coming soon.

B OK. You can tell them what _____

_____ (happen).

2 Put either **for** or **since** with these time expressions.

a. _____ a long time

b. _____ ten days

c. _____ my last birthday

d. _____ the end of the holidays

e. _____ ages

f. _____ I came to England

g. _____ the last few days

h. _____ the day I met you

i. _____ the beginning of the lesson

3 Here is an advertisement for a car.

FORD CORTINA 1980
Red, One owner. Good condition.
35,000 miles. No accidents. £2000

Write a question for each item of information.

a. What sort *of car is it?*

b. How _____

c. What _____

d. How many _____

e. What sort _____

f. How many _____

g. _____

h. _____

4 Barry and James are talking about cars. Complete the conversation.

Barry *Have you got a car, James?*
James Yes, I have.

Barry What _____ ,
James It's a Volvo.

Barry _____
James I've had it for eighteen months, I think.

Barry _____
James £5,500. It was second-hand, not new.

Barry _____
James It hasn't done a lot, actually. About 10,000. I only use it at weekends.

Barry _____
James In 1971. I passed first time. I was lucky.

Barry _____
James Yes, I have. It was a rainy evening last November, and I skidded into the car in front. Nobody was hurt, fortunately.

5 You have applied for these jobs. Say why you think you should get the job.

Accountant
I've always been good at figures. I worked as an accountant from 1978 to 1980. I've read a lot of books about accountancy. I like working in an office.

a. Tourist guide for your town or country

_____

_____

_____

b. Hotel manager

_____

_____

_____

c. Chef

_____

_____

_____

_____

6 Complete the sentences by matching a line from column **A** with a line from column **B**.

A
a. Jane's angry because
b. Anne's disappointed because
c. Julie's excited because
d. Kate's jealous because
e. Mary's worried because

B
1 she hasn't heard from her parents for a long time, and hopes they're all right.
2 she's just seen someone in the kind of car that she wants to buy.
3 her boyfriend hasn't arrived and they're already late for the party.
4 she's just won first prize in a competition.
5 she's had to cancel her holiday, and she was so looking forward to it.

a ____ b ____ c ____ d ____ e ____

7 **Vocabulary**

Look at the dictionary entries on the next page and complete the sentences.

a. If we want a holiday this year we'll have to

_____ . We're spending too much.

b. Every country has its own _____ problems

c. She's an _____ lecturer at Glasgow University.

d. The most _____ way of heating your house is by using solar energy.

e. The Chancellor of the Exchequer is the minister

responsible for the _____ .

f. Naturally he has many professional _____

_____ to advise him.

g. The world _____ situation gets more and more complicated.

h. It is usually more _____ to shop in a supermarket than in a small shop.

i. He presented himself very well at the interview. He

was very professional and _____ .

j. Would you like a cup of coffee or shall we _____

_____ straight away?

21

k. A How much do you earn a year, Dad?
   B That's nothing to do with you. _____

   _____.

l. Peter's thinking of _____ the textile business when he leaves university.

m. I have to go abroad _____ for at least two months a year.

n. In a hotel, it is a receptionist's business _____

   _____.

8 Write the letter of application for one of the jobs in Exercise 5. Include any information you think relevant. Think particularly about

your education and qualifications;

any experience relevant to the job;

why you are interested in the job;

when you are available for interview.

Look at page 29 of the Students' Book to remind yourself of the conventions of formal letter writing. Pay attention to your choice of tense.

_____
_____
_____
_____
_____
_____

Dear   ,
I would like to apply for the post of _____

_____, *which I saw advertised in _____*

_____
_____
_____
_____
_____
_____
_____
_____
_____
_____
_____
_____
_____
_____
_____
_____
_____
_____
_____
_____

---

econ·omic /ˌiːkəˈnɒmɪk US: ˌek-/ adj **1** of economics (⇨ below): *the government's ~ policy.* **2** designed to give a profit: *an ~ rent,* one that compensates the owner for the cost of the land, building, etc. **3** connected with commerce and industry: *~ geography,* studied chiefly in connection with industry.

econ·omi·cal /ˌiːkəˈnɒmɪkl US: ˌek-/ adj careful in the spending of money, time, etc and in the use of goods; not wasteful: *to be ~ of time and energy; an ~ fire,* one that does not waste fuel. **~·ly** /-klɪ/ adv

econ·omics /ˌiːkəˈnɒmɪks US: ˌek-/ n (with sing v) [U] science of the production, distribution and consumption of goods; condition of a country as to material prosperity. **econ·om·ist** /ɪˈkɒnəmɪst/ n **1** expert in ~; person who writes or lectures on ~ or political economy. **2** person who is economical or thrifty.

econ·om·ize /ɪˈkɒnəmaɪz/ vt,vi [VP6A,2A,3A] ~ **(on sth),** be economical; use or spend less than before; cut down expenses: *He ~d by using buses instead of taking taxis. We must ~ on light and fuel.*

econ·omy /ɪˈkɒnəmɪ/ n (pl -mies) **1** [C,U] (instance of) avoidance of waste of money, strength or anything else of value: *to practise ~. In the long run, it is an ~ to buy good quality goods, even though they cost more. By various little economies, she managed to save enough money for a holiday.* **'~ class,** cheapest class of travel (esp by air). **2** [U] control and management of the money, goods and other resources of a community, society or household: *political ~; domestic ~.* **3** [C] system for the management and use of resources: *the totalitarian economies of Germany and Italy before the Second World War.*

---

busi·ness /ˈbɪznɪs/ n **1** [U] buying and selling; commerce; trade: *We do not do much ~ with them. He's in the wool ~,* buys and sells wool. *He has set up in ~ as a bookseller. He is in ~ for himself,* works on his own account, is not employed by others. *Which do you want to do, go into ~ or become a lawyer?* **on ~,** for the purpose of doing ~: *Are you here on ~ or for pleasure?* **'~ address,** address of one's shop, office, etc. Cf home address. **'~ hours,** hours during which ~ is done, eg 9am to 5pm. **'~-like** adj using, showing system, promptness, care, etc. **'~·man** /-mæn/ n (pl -men) man who is engaged in buying and selling, etc. **2** [C] shop; commercial enterprise, etc: *He has a good ~ as a greengrocer. He is the manager of three different ~es. The newspapers advertise many small ~es for sale.* **3** [U] task, duty, concern; what has to be done: *It is a teacher's ~ to help his pupils. I will make it my ~ (= will undertake) to see that the money is paid promptly. That's no ~ of yours,* is something about which you need not or should not trouble. **get down to ~,** start the work that must be done. **mind one's own ~,** attend to one's own duties and not interfere with those of others. **mean ~,** be in earnest. **send sb about his ~,** send him away and tell him not to interfere. **4** [U] right:

22

UNIT 8

Obligation

1 Put an appropriate verb of obligation in its correct form into each gap. The verbs are **must, have to, had to, have had to, should**.
The forms are positive, negative, and gerund.

a. I really do think you _____ get your hair cut.

b. Careful, darling. You _____ play with matches. They're too dangerous.

c. My wife suddenly became ill in the middle of the night and I _____ call the doctor.

d. I'm overweight. The doctor said I _____ eat too many sweets or potatoes.

e. I like Saturdays because I _____ get up early.

f. **A** Why have you got so much money on you? You _____ keep it in the bank.

B I know. But today's the day I _____ pay my employees.

g. It's my mother's birthday next week. I _____ remember to buy her a present and a card.

h. No one likes _____ work at week-ends.

i. You _____ come with me if you don't want to. I don't mind going on my own. You _____ stay here if you like.

j. I have a really bad memory for phone numbers. I _____ look them up in the book every time.

k. When I was at school we _____ wear a uniform. Everybody hated it.

l. You _____ touch electrical applicances if you've got wet hands. You could kill yourself.

m. She has a private income. She _____ never _____ do one day's work in the whole of her life.

2 **Social rules**
You are in Britain. A British friend of similar age and background to yourself has invited you home for a meal.
Choose the best answer, a, b, c, or d, about how you should behave. There is not necessarily one best answer.

1 When you go to their house, should you
   a. take some flowers?
   b. take some wine?
   c. take a present for their children?
   d. ask them before what they would like you to bring?

2 When you arrive and meet the other guests, should you
   a. introduce yourself to the other guests?
   b. shake hands with all the other guests?
   c. wait to be introduced to the other guests by your hosts?
   d. tell everyone your name, job, and position in your company?

3 You would like to look round their house. Should you
   a. wait to be invited?
   b. ask if you can look round?
   c. go and look round without saying anything?
   d. ask the wife of the house to show you round?

4 Some food is served that you really don't like. Should you say
   a. 'I'll just have a little bit, please'?
   b. 'I'd rather not have any of that, thank you'?
   c. 'I'm awfully sorry. I don't like that'?
   d. nothing, and eat it?

5 In the days after the invitation, should you
   a. write your hosts a thank-you letter?
   b. phone them to say thank you?
   c. invite them to your house or to a restaurant?
   d. not get in touch at all?

3 What are your opinions on the following issues? What advice would you give to those concerned?

   a. A parent has found drugs in the possession of his teenage child.

   _____

   _____

   _____

   _____

   b. Unemployment in the world. There will probably never be full employment again.

   _____

   _____

   _____

   _____

   c. Soon more than half the world's population will be over 65 years of age.

   _____

   _____

   _____

   _____

   _____

4 **Sentence stress**
   In the following dialogues, one word in Speaker B's sentence will normally be stressed more than the other words. Underline which word you think it is.

   A I wonder why they live in such a horrible place.
   B I suppose they <u>like</u> it there.

   a. **A** I love reading a good book before going to sleep.
      B So do I.
   b. **A** You'd have more money if your wife went out to work.
      B She does go out to work.

   c. **A** I didn't know Sheila and Bertrand were getting married!
      B But I told you.
   d. **A** When did you tell me that?
      B I told you yesterday.
   e. **A** Are they getting married before the summer?
      B No. They're getting married after the summer.

5 **Vocabulary:** Feeling ill
   This is the story of someone's short illness. Look up any words you don't know in the dictionary, and put the sentences in the right order.

   a. The following morning I still didn't feel any better, so I went down to the surgery.
   b. When I woke up on Tuesday I felt sick and dizzy.
   c. It cleared up the sore throat very quickly.
   d. I was shivering one minute and sweating the next.
   e. I started feeling ill on Monday evening. I had a bit of a temperature, so I took an aspirin and had an early night.
   f. When I saw the doctor I explained my symptoms.
   g. I took the prescription to the chemist, where I got an antibiotic.
   h. He examined me, and said I had the 'flu and a sore throat.
   i. I took things easy, and by the weekend I had completely recovered.
   j. He gave me a prescription for the sore throat, and said that I should go to bed for a few days.
   k. I had some toast, but I was sick immediately, so I went back to bed. I had a fever.

   1 ☐   2 ☐   3 ☐   4 ☐   5 ☐
   6 ☐   7 ☐   8 ☐   9 ☐   10 ☐
   11 ☐

6 **Vocabulary:** People in the medical profession
   What do these people do?

   a nurse
   A nurse looks after patients in hospital.

   a. a surgeon

   _____

   b. a sister

   _____

   c. a consultant

   _____

   d. a midwife

   _____

   e. a dentist

   _____

7 An English friend is going to spend some time in your country. Write a dialogue between yourself and your friend. The friend asks questions, and you reply and give advice, about the following subjects:

— what clothes to take
— what areas to visit
— general advice and warnings
— where to stay
— what food to try
— what medical precautions to take

Friend *I'm going to spend some time in your country. Can you give me some advice?*
You *What would you like to know?*

Friend *Well,* _____

_____

_____

_____

_____

_____

_____

_____

_____

_____

_____

_____

_____

_____

_____

_____

_____

_____

_____

_____

_____

_____

_____

UNIT 9

Conditionals

1 Put the verb in brackets into the correct tense for a clause of condition or result. There are examples of the first, second, and zero conditionals.

a. If you _____ (go) away, please write to me.

b. If my wife _____ (be) as violent as yours, I _____ (leave) her.

c. If it _____ (rain) this weekend, we _____ (not able) to play tennis.

d. If I _____ (see) Peter this afternoon, I _____ (tell) him the news.

e. I _____ (not like) meat if it _____ _____ (be) undercooked. I prefer it well done.

f. Please start your meal. If you _____ (not have) your soup now, it _____ (go) cold.

g. I have to work about 80 hours a week. If I _____ _____ (have) more time, I _____ _____ (take up) a sport like tennis.

h. If he _____ (be) taller, he _____ _____ (can) be a policeman, but he's too short.

2 Why do you go to these places?
You go to a lost property office if *you've lost something./you lose something.*

a. You go to a heel bar if _____ _____

b. You go to a casualty department if _____ _____

c. You go to a registry office if _____ _____

d. You go to a betting shop if _____ _____

e. You go to a Chinese take-away if _____ _____

3 Is your country run as you would like it?
Complete the sentence by matching a line from column **A** with a line from column **B**.

A
a. ☐ If I were Minister of the Environment,
b. ☐ If I were Minister of Defence,
c. ☐ If I were Minister of Trade,
d. ☐ If I were in charge of the Home Office,
e. ☐ If I were Minister of Finance,

B
1 I'd ban the import of foreign cars.
2 I'd increase tax on people with very high incomes.
3 I'd stop factories letting harmful chemicals into the atmosphere.
4 I'd bring back the death penalty.
5 I'd build up conventional weapons and get rid of nuclear weapons.

What changes would *you* make if you were Minister of various departments? What would be the results of these changes?

If I were in charge of the Home Office, I'd reduce the number of prisoners, because if there were fewer prisoners, we wouldn't need so many prisons.

Finance

_____
_____
_____
_____
_____
_____
_____

Trade

_____
_____
_____
_____
_____
_____
_____

Defence

_____
_____
_____
_____
_____
_____
_____

Are there any other areas where changes would be desirable?

_____
_____
_____
_____
_____

4 Vocabulary: Make and do

Write in **make** or **do**. Unfortunately there are no rules to guide you.

____ a mistake	____ a will	____ a complaint
____ progress	____ friends with	____ up my mind to . . .
____ someone a favour	____ business with	____ nothing
____ a speech	____ a noise	____ sense
____ my home-work	____ a phone call	____ a mess
____ one's best	____ sure that . . .	____ the house-work
____ money	____ an exam	

Complete these sentences, using one of the above in an appropriate form.

a. Could you _____? Could you give me a lift to the station?

b. At first I found English difficult, but now I'm

beginning _____.

c. Customer to waiter: 'I think you _____. My bill should be £5, not £15.'

d. I _____ a lot of _____ with the Chinese. They are good customers of mine.

e. Can you understand these instructions? They

_____ to me.

f. It took me a long time to decide, but I have

finally _____ to accept the job.

g. Sh! Don't _____. The baby's asleep.

h. Hello. I'd like _____. There's no hot water in my room.

i. Before going on holiday you should _____

_____ all windows and doors are shut and locked.

j. **A:** You must try harder.

   B: I'm _____
   A: Well, it's not good enough.

k. Yesterday the Prime Minister _____ in the House of Commons.

l. It took me hours to clean your room. If you

_____ again, you can clean it up yourself.

m. Is there a public call box near here? I need to

_____.

27

5 Henry is selling his old car. He is trying to come to an arrangement with Chris.

Chris How much do you want for it?
Henry Five hundred pounds.
Chris I'll give you three hundred.
Henry Don't be silly. It's worth much more than that!
Chris OK. I'll give you four hundred if you repair the engine.
Henry If I could repair the engine, I wouldn't sell it. I'd keep it for myself.
Chris Four hundred and fifty. My final offer.
Henry All right. It's yours.

Write similar dialogues.

a. **Salesman** and **customer**

A salesman is trying to persuade a customer to buy solar panels for his house. His heating bills would be smaller, his neighbours would be impressed. The customer isn't interested.

b. **Parent** and **child**

The child wants an increase in pocket money, but the parent insists on certain conditions.

UNIT 10

Ability and Permission

1 Put an appropriate verb in its correct form into each gap.
The verbs are **can, could, to be able**.
The forms are positive and negative.

a. In my country you _____ get married when you are 16.

b. Women _____ vote in England until 1922.

c. Last night I _____ get into my house because I had forgotten my key.

d. I phoned the Gas Board because I thought I

_____ smell gas, which is very dangerous.

e. 'Hello. Is that the dentist? _____ I make an appointment to see you, please?'

f. I'm learning car mechanics because I want

_____ to service my own car. It costs a fortune if you send it to the garage.

g. Many night animals _____ see very well, but they have a highly developed sense of smell.

h. If you _____ do this exercise, you're very clever!

2 **Social situations**
Write what you would say in the following situations.

a. You are in a crowded restaurant. You see a table with one chair free. What do you ask the other people at the table before you sit down?

_____

_____

_____

b. You are at a friend's house. You have to make a short, but very urgent phone call. What do you say?

_____

_____

c. Your landlord has come to collect the rent, but you have no money. Apologize, and offer to pay tomorrow.

_____

_____

d. You have to fill in a form, but haven't got a pen. Ask to borrow one.

_____

_____

3 On this page there are two separate dialogues, but they are mixed up. Sort them out and put them in the right order.

In Dialogue 1, Mr Roberts and Mr Thomas are talking in an office.
In Dialogue 2, a father and son are talking.

a. But I'm taking Dave to see his girlfriend in hospital.
b. Yes, what is it?
c. I told you. I need it.
d. It's not a very convenient time at the moment.
e. Well, as you know, my father can't walk very well, and he needs to go into hospital. I was wondering if I could have a day off work?
f. Thanks a lot, Dad. I won't be home late.
g. Oh, please. He won't be able to go if I don't give him a lift.
h. That's very kind. I'll make up the time, I promise.
i. No, you can't. I need it.
j. Mr Roberts? Could I have a word with you?

k. I'd be terribly grateful. He wouldn't be able to go if I wasn't there to help him.

l. All right. I suppose I can walk. The exercise will do me good.

m. Well, if that's the case I suppose you should.

n. Dad, can I have the car tonight?

Dialogue 1 | **Dialogue 2**

Dialogue 1	Dialogue 2
☐ Mr Thomas	☐ Son
☐ Mr Roberts	☐ Father
☐ Mr Thomas	☐ Son
☐ Mr Roberts	☐ Father
☐ Mr Thomas	☐ Son
☐ Mr Roberts	☐ Father
☐ Mr Thomas	☐ Son

In both dialogues, one person is asking for permission and the other is giving permission. Compare the differences.

I was wondering if I could have a day off work?
Can I have the car tonight?

4 Word formation

These suffixes are used to form nouns.

– ion   – ment   – tion   – ance   – ssion

Below is a list of words that appeared in the article about Ruth on page 56 of the Students' Book. They were in either their noun or verb form. Use your dictionary to find the nouns for these verbs. They all have one of the above suffixes, and they have the stress on the last-but-one syllable. Mark the stress.

Verb	Noun
explain	*explan'ation*
enjoy	
expect	
achieve	
satisfy	
require	
admit	
disappoint	
excite	

These suffixes are used to signify a person.

- ian   - er   - ist

These suffixes are used to signify the subjects they study.

- y   - ics

Below is a list of subjects, the person that studies them, and the adjective. Use your dictionary to fill in the chart. Mark the stress. Be very careful. The stress often changes from one syllable to another in the same word. Add some words of your own.

Subject	Person	Adjective
'history	his'torian	his'torical
	mathema'tician	
	'chemist	
'science		
		'physical
bi'ology		
phi'losophy		
	psy'chologist	
		me'chanical
'music		
	'architect	
arche'ology		

5 Put these expressions in order of ability.

1 = best.   6 = worst.

☐ I did well at maths.
☐ I was hopeless at maths.
☐ I was very good at maths.
☐ I knew absolutely nothing about maths.
☐ I was best at maths.
☐ I was quite good at maths.

Put these sentences in order of preference.

1 = most liked.   7 = least liked.

☐ I liked maths.
☐ I disliked maths.
☐ I hated maths.
☐ I loved maths.
☐ I didn't mind maths.
☐ I couldn't stand maths.
☐ Maths was my favourite subject.

6 Write a short paragraph about the subjects you liked and disliked at school.

_____

_____

_____

_____

_____

_____

Revision

1 Here is a passage about Britain and the monarchy. There are twenty gaps. Some gaps have a verb in brackets. Put the verb in the correct tense.

Yesterday I *went* (go) to the park.

When there is no verb in brackets, put in ONE suitable word — perhaps a preposition, an adverb, a modal verb, etc.

I came *to* London to learn English.

Contractions such as **won't, can't** count as one word.

Britain, as I am sure you know, is a monarchy.

England (a) _____ (have) a king or

queen (b) _____ over a thousand years.

One of the (c) _____ famous was

Henry VIII, who (d) _____ (become)

king in 1506 and reigned (e) _____ 1547. He broke away from the Roman Catholic Church

so that he (f) _____ divorce and marry again.

Elizabeth II (g) _____ (be) on the throne

(h) _____ 1952, and is generally very popular. I think she has quite an unenviable job. She

(i) _____ to meet a lot of people who she probably does not want to talk to, and keep smiling. How awful! Some people think she (j)

_____ give up the throne because she

(k) _____ (rule) for such a long time.

It's quite possible. If she (l) _____ (do),

Prince Charles (m) _____ become king.

I (n) _____ (read) a lot about the royal family recently, as there has been so much in the press

about them. You (o) _____ open a newspaper without seeing a picture of one of them. People are fascinated to know what they are (p)

_____ as people, what they do, and everything about their private lives. I often wonder

what Prince Charles (q) _____ do if he

(r) _____ (not be) the Queen's son. I

suppose he (s) _____ (make) a lot of money in business, or something like that. Anyway,

I'm sure he (t) _____ be a very good king.

2 Use the suggestions in the right-hand column and your own ideas to complete this dialogue.

Peter is the Director of an English Language School, Chrissy is the Director of Studies.

Peter How many teachers have we got working here at the moment?
Chrissy Twenty-five. Why?
Peter I think we are going to need some more.

_____	Fifteen new
_____	students enrolled
_____	for next month.
_____	Group from France,
_____	special classes.
_____	Need two teachers.
Chrissy _____	Advertisement,
_____	newspaper.

Peter I don't think we have time for that. We'll need these people quite soon.
Chrissy Actually, I know someone who would be very good. Her name's Alison Roberts.
Peter What's she like?

Chrissy _____	Reliable, hard-
_____	working. Gets
_____	on well with

_____ people.

_____ Experienced –

_____ taught for six

_____ years.

Peter Where has she taught
before?

Chrissy _____ Egypt, Spain.

_____ Special courses,

_____ business people.

_____ Written a book.

_____ Trained with me,

_____ 1978.

Peter I think I know her. What
does she look like?

Chrissy _____ Physical descrip-

_____ tion, age,

_____ clothes, accent,

_____ very amusing.

_____ (Use the picture

_____ on the right as

_____ a cue.)

_____

_____

_____

Peter She sounds very good.
Can you get in touch with her?

Chrissy She sometimes comes to
my flat. If _____ she/tonight,

_____ I/tell her

Peter Yes, please.

3 Re-read page 40 of the Students' Book.

Try to guess the meaning of the words in italics, which
you probably don't know. Can you guess exactly?
approximately? not at all?

a. It was a cold day and we had a long walk in front
   of us. Before setting out, we made some
   sandwiches and poured some hot soup into a
   vacuum flask.

b. When I am painting someone's portrait, I like to do
   several quick *sketches* in pencil before beginning
   the actual picture. It helps me to practise the
   angles.

c. We didn't have a fridge, so we had to eat food
   quite soon after buying it or it would *go off*, and
   that's a terrible waste.

d. My next-door neighbour wanted me to repair her
   washing machine, so I took the tools I thought I'd
   need – hammer, screw-driver, and *spanners* of
   various sizes.

e. 'I'm terribly sorry I'm late. I had an awful journey
   here. I was driving along when I heard this huge
   explosion. I thought someone was *firing* a gun at
   me, then the car started going all over the road and
   I realized I had a *puncture*. I had a *spare wheel*, so
   that was all right, but when I opened the *boot* I
   couldn't find the *jack*, so there was nothing I could
   do. I came here by taxi.'

f. James was not enjoying the party. He disliked all
   social occasions where people had to mix and
   exchange *small talk*. But one woman caught his
   eye. She was *overdressed*, in James's opinion. Her
   clothes had been chosen to look expensive. She
   wore a lot of jewellery – her necklace and ear-
   rings *sparkled*, and when she waved her arms,
   which she often did in a dramatic way, her *bangles*
   rattled.

UNIT 11

Present Perfect Continuous

1 Put the verb in brackets in the correct tense, Present Perfect Simple or Present Perfect Continuous.

a. I'm exhausted. I _____ (work) all day, and I _____ (not finish) yet.

b. I _____ (visit) many countries in the last five years.

c. Someone ____ _____ (take) my books. I _____ (look) for them for ages, but I can't find them anywhere.

d. I _____ (shop) all morning, but I _____ (not buy) anything yet. I haven't seen anything I've liked.

e. The best book I _____ ever _____ (read) is *One Hundred Years of Solitude* by Gabriel Marquez.

f. **A** You're filthy! What _____ you _____ (do)?

   B I _____ (work) in the garden. I _____ (plant) all the vegetables for next year.

g. I _____ (wait) for two hours, but nobody _____ (arrive) yet.

2 Put the verb in the correct tense. Choose from the Present Perfect Simple or the Present Perfect Continuous; or the Present Simple or Present Continuous.

I *have been learning* (learn) Italian for the past three years, but there's still a lot I *don't understand* (not understand).

a. **A** Oh dear! Look out of the window. It _____ _____ (rain).

   B Oh no. I _____ (not bring) my umbrella.

b. My uncle _____ (know) everything about roses. He _____ (grow) them for 35 years. Now he _____ (try) to produce a blue one.

c. I _____ (listen) to you for the past half an hour, but I'm afraid I _____ (not understand) a word.

d. **A** What's the matter, Jane?

   B I _____ (read) in my room and the light isn't very good. I _____ (have) a headache. It's really hurting.

3 Write two sentences about what these people have been doing.
My mother's coming to stay for a week.
I've been tidying the house.
I've been getting her bedroom ready.

a. They moved into their new house last week.

_____

_____

b. Tom is saving up to buy a new car.

_____

_____

c. I'm trying to lose weight.

_____

_____

4 Look up the words in italics in your dictionary, and write a sentence explaining what has been happening.

She's got a lovely *tan*.
She's been lying in the sun.

a. He's *panting*.

_____

b. Jack's putting away the *lawn mower*.

_____

c. My car is *gleaming*.

_____

d. The roads are *flooded*.

_____

e. I feel *dizzy*.

_____

f. You smell of *bonfires*.

_____

g. Why have you got *glue* all over your fingers?

_____

5 Here is a profile of a company. *One* word is missing from each statement. Indicate where the word should be, and write the word in the right-hand column.

e.g. *TOP is one of* ⋀ *world's biggest producers of chemicals.*   *the*

Roof Tex is a small company produces roof tiles. It is based in   _____

Heddington, a small town in the south of England, and it been   _____

operating for twenty years. Offices were in central London, but   _____

they have recently moved to the factory site. It twenty-five   _____

workers and has a sales staff five. Some of the employees have   _____

been for the company since it started. Raw materials are supplied   _____

by a nearby quarry. The company has using the services of a local   _____

transport firm for the distribution of its. It has one competitor   _____

that has tried several to take the company over.   _____

6 Write a short profile of a company. Include information such as what it does, where it is, how many people it employs, and how it operates.

_____

_____

_____

_____

_____

_____

_____

_____

_____

_____

_____

_____

_____

_____

_____

_____

7 **Compound words**

reading	Christmas	telephone	egg
football	writing	tea	birthday
washing	recipe	medicine	wrapping
hot water	sun	sewing	wellington

Put each of the above words with one of the nouns below to form a compound. Check in your dictionary to see if they are one word, two words, or hyphenated.

_____ cup	_____ paper
_____ cup	_____ paper
_____ glasses	_____ bottle
_____ glasses	_____ bottle
_____ book	_____ machine
_____ book	_____ machine
_____ card	_____ boots
_____ card	_____ boots

34

Choose some of the compounds above and write a sentence to explain what they are.
You wear sun-glasses to protect your eyes from the sun.

_____

_____

_____

_____

_____

_____

Write a sentence to illustrate the meaning of these words.
the Highway code
You must know the Highway Code to pass your test.

to overtake

_____

a traffic jam

_____

to reverse

_____

a speed limit

_____

a dual carriageway

_____

a service station

_____

8 **Vocabulary:** cars and driving
Put the correct numbers in the boxes.

1 steering-wheel
2 windscreen
3 brake
4 door handle
5 handbrake
6 gear stick
7 windscreen wiper
8 accelerator
9 horn
10 indicator switch
11 clutch
12 rear-view mirror
13 light switch
14 seat belt

1 boot
2 blinkers
3 headlight
4 spare wheel
5 bumper
6 number plate
7 wheel
8 bonnet
9 sidelight
10 tyre

UNIT 12

Making Arrangements/Expressing Degrees of Future Certainty

	Morning	Afternoon	Evening
Monday	Dentist 10·00	Shopping	Guests for dinner
Tuesday	Travel agent – book tickets	Art gallery	Cinema 7·00
Wednesday	Plumber coming to fix washing machine	Anna's house 3·00	Packing
Thursday	Fly to Italy		

1 Look at Kate's diary.

Friends ring to invite her out, but of course, she has to refuse.

A *Would you like to | come round for coffee on*
      Why don't you | Monday morning?
Kate *That's very kind, but I'm afraid I'm going to the dentist then.*

Write similar dialogues. Friends invite Kate to play tennis/go to the theatre/go out for a meal, etc. Kate refuses, and says what she's doing at that time.

a. **A** _____

   Kate _____

b. **A** _____

   Kate _____

c. **A** _____

   Kate _____

d. **A** _____

   Kate _____

e. **A** _____

   Kate _____

f. **A** _____

   Kate _____

g. **A** _____

   Kate _____

2 Look at these dialogues.

rain tomorrow? (✓)

A *Do you think it'll rain tomorrow?*
B *Yes, I think it probably will. The weather forecast isn't very good.*

James / win / tennis championship? (X)

A *Do you think James will win the tennis championship?*

B *Well, he might, but I doubt it. He hasn't been playing very well recently.*

Write similar dialogues. Add a reason to support B's opinion.

a. you / pass / exam? (X)

A _____

B _____

b. Peter / get / promotion he wants? (✓)

A _____

B _____

c. there / be / nuclear war? (X)

A _____

B _____

d. we / find / cure for cancer? (✓)

A _____

B _____

3 These dialogues are a little different. Be careful with the word order in the question.

When / you / be / back home?
6.00.

A *When do you think you'll be back home?*

B *I might be back at 6.00. It depends on the traffic.*

Write similar dialogues. Add a reason to support B's opinion.

a. How / you / find / money to buy a car?
Bank loan.

A _____

B _____

b. When / your book / be / ready for publication?
In six months' time.

A _____

B _____

c. Who / get job of Director?
Henry.

A _____

B _____

d. How long / your trip around the world / take you?
A couple of years.

A _____

B _____

4 Write similar predictions on these subjects. Give reasons to support your opinions.

Who do you think will win the next elections in your country?

_____
_____
_____
_____
_____
_____
_____
_____

What do you think you'll do after you've finished this course?

_____
_____
_____
_____
_____
_____
_____
_____
_____
_____

5 **Phrasal verbs**

Complete these sentences with the verb **look** in an appropriate form, and choose the correct preposition or adverb.

after	for	out	forward to	up

a. Baby-sitters are people who _____

b. I wonder what 'scratch' means. I'll _____ dictionary.

c. **A** What are you doing on your hands and knees?

   B I _____ my glasses. Have you seen them anywhere?

d. Look _____! That box is going to fall on your head!

e. It's a great pleasure to meet you. I've heard a lot about you, and I _____ meeting you for a long time.

37

6 Replace the verbs in these sentences with the verb **put** and the correct preposition or adverb.

away   back   off   out   up with

Then replace the words in italics with a pronoun.

He placed *the money* on the table.
He put the money down on the table.
He put it down on the table.

a. It is difficult to extinguish *electrical fires*.

_____

_____

b. I don't know how you can tolerate *so much noise*.

_____

_____

c. Please replace *the books* on the shelves.

_____

_____

d. We have postponed *the meeting* until next week.

_____

_____

e. Could you please tidy *all your clothes*?

_____

_____

7 **Vocabulary:** animals

Which animal . . .?
wags its tail and fetches sticks
a dog

a. has fur and whiskers, and catches mice

_____

b. has a beak and feathers, and builds nests

_____

c. has horns and is dangerous

_____

d. is supposed to be the King of the Jungle

_____

e. has a reputation for being stubborn

_____

f. has gills and fins

_____

g. can imitate human voices

_____

h. is the emblem of peace

_____

i. sometimes poisons, and sometimes squeezes to death its victims

_____

j. is the largest in the world

_____

k. lives in a stable and wears a saddle

_____

l. eats honey and is a popular soft toy for children

_____

Which animal . . .?
m. purrs

_____

n. barks

_____

o. roars

_____

p. hisses

_____

UNIT 13

The Passive

1 Compare these sentences.

People speak English all over the world.
English is spoken all over the world.

In the passive, the agent (in this sentence 'people') is often unnecessary. Put these sentences into the passive. *By* + agent is not necessary.

a. The postman delivers the letters at 8.00.

_____

b. Someone built this hotel two years ago.

_____

c. They use a lot of preservatives in food these days.

_____

d. Has anyone answered your question?

_____

e. Somebody found your keys on top of the photocopier.

_____

f. People should not take reference books out of the library.

_____

g. They have increased the rate of taxation to forty per cent.

_____

h. A scientist discovered penicillin in 1928.

_____

2 Put the verb in brackets in the correct form, active or passive, and also in the correct tense.

Last night a man *was arrested* (arrest) outside Buckingham Palace. Police *saw* (see) him climbing the walls.

A Have you heard the news today?
B No, why?

A Well, the police (a) _____ (arrest) Ronald Bloggs.

B Who's he?
A He was one of the men who (b) _____

_____ (rob) a train in Britain about thirty years ago.
B Good Lord! I remember that. It was one of the biggest robberies ever. How much money (c) _____

_____ (steal)?

A Millions. And it (d) _____

(never find). Bloggs (e) _____

(send) to prison but he (f) _____

_____ (escape). Anyway, he

(g) _____ (arrest) _____

yesterday. He (h) _____ (live) in Brazil for the past fifteen years, and the British police have been trying all this time to bring him back, but they can't, because Britain doesn't have an extradition treaty with Brazil.

B So who (i) _____ (arrest) him, the British police or the Brazilian police?

A The Brazilian police. Apparently he (j) _____

_____ (catch) shoplifting. He put something in his pocket, and he didn't know that a store

detective (k) _____ (watch) him.
B But why is this in all the press? It's not very important, is it?
A Because now he will have a criminal record, and

under Brazilian law he could (l) _____

_____ (send) back to Britain. If that happened, he

would (m) _____ (imprison) here to finish his sentence.

3 This is the story of Joe, an unsuccessful burglar.

The sentences are not in the right order. There are probably some words that you don't know. Look them up in your dictionary, and put the sentences in the right order.

a. ☐ He was arrested.
b. ☐ He was found guilty.
c. ☐ Joe broke into a shop.
d. ☐ He came before the Magistrates' Court.
e. ☐ He was taken to the police station.
f. ☐ The police arrived to investigate.
g. ☐ He was seen breaking in and the police were called.
h. ☐ He was fined two hundred pounds and given a two-year suspended sentence.
i. ☐ He was given bail.
j. ☐ He was questioned.
k. ☐ He was caught as he was escaping.
l. ☐ He was charged with robbery.

4 Rewrite the story above as it might appear in a newspaper. You will need to make a lot of changes. Use your imagination to fill in details. Give the article a title.

_____

In the Magistrates' Court yesterday, Joseph Bills, a 35-year-old unemployed builder, was found guilty of

robbery. _____

_____

_____

_____

_____

_____

_____

_____

_____

_____

5 **Vocabulary:** crime

Fill in the columns. Add some crimes yourself.

Crime	Criminal	Verb
burglary		
robbery		
	murderer	
		to kidnap
	shoplifter	
mugging		
	smuggler	
		to hijack
	blackmailer	
vandalism		

Choose some of the above crimes. Write a few sentences saying in each case what the criminal is trying to do, and how.

A kidnapper takes a person, sometimes a child, to get money from the family. When the family pays the ransom, the person is set free.

_____

_____

_____

_____

_____

_____

_____

_____

_____

_____

_____

_____

6 Describing processes

What happens to a letter between the time it is posted and the time it is delivered?

_____

_____

_____

_____

_____

_____

_____

_____

_____

_____

_____

_____

_____

What happens to you, your ticket, your luggage, etc. when you go to an airport to catch a plane?

_____

_____

_____

_____

_____

_____

_____

_____

_____

_____

_____

_____

UNIT 14

Reported Speech

1 Report these words and thoughts using the verb suggested.

a. 'I'm going to Paris soon.'

She said _____

b. 'It's time to start revising for the exam,' said the teacher.

The teacher told _____

_____

c. 'The film will be interesting.'

I thought _____

_____

d. 'I can't help you because I have too much to do.'

She said _____

_____

e. 'Anne has bought the tickets.'

I was told _____

_____

f. 'It took me three hours to get here because the roads are flooded.'

He told me _____

_____

g. 'I think it's a crazy idea. It won't work.'

She said _____

_____

h. 'Breakfast is served between 7.00 and 9.00.'

The receptionist explained _____

_____

2 Put one of the following verbs in its correct form into each gap.

say   tell   explain   speak   talk   reply

I met Mr Brown in the street the other day, and we

stopped and (a) _____ for a while.

He (b) _____ me that his wife had been taken into hospital. When I asked him how she was,

he (c) _____ that she was getting better. He wondered why I hadn't been to the tennis club for

a few months, so I (d) _____ that I'd been very busy lately and just hadn't had time.

'There's something you must (e) _____ me,' he said. 'How many languages can your son

(f) _____?'

'Four,' I (g) _____. 'Why?' 'I know your son has some very funny stories to

(h) _____ about learning languages and living abroad. We're having a meeting of the Travellers Club next week, and I'd like him to

(i) _____ at it.'

I (j) _____ I would (k) _____ to my son about it, and promised to get back in touch.

Then we (l) _____ goodbye and went our separate ways.

3 For the following verbs that introduce reported commands, write an appropriate sentence in direct speech, then report it.

warn

'Be careful of strangers and don't go out at night.'
He warned me to be careful of strangers and not to go
out at night.

a. advise

_____

_____

b. remind

_____

_____

c. invite

_____

_____

d. ask

_____

_____

e. tell

_____

_____

f. persuade

_____

_____

g. urge

_____

_____

4 Report these words and thoughts, using the verbs
suggested.

a. 'Where are you going?'

He asked me _____

_____

b. 'Do you want to go out for a meal?'

She asked him _____

_____

c. 'Why are you late?' they asked their guest.

They wondered _____

_____

d. 'Can I use your phone to make a local call?'

She asked me _____

e. 'Which countries have you been to?'

The customs officer asked me _____

_____

f. 'Do you know where Angela is living?'

He asked me _____

_____

g. 'What colour are you going to paint the living
room?'

She asked them _____

_____

h. 'Why doesn't she talk to me any more?' I thought
to myself.

I wondered why _____

_____

5 Imagine you overheard these conversations in a
restaurant. In your curiosity, what other information
would you like to know?

'He earns over one hundred thousand pounds a year.'
I wonder what his job is.
I wonder what he spends it on.
I'd love to know where he lives.

a. 'She's had so many husbands, she forgets their
names.'

_____

_____

_____

b. 'I've never worked a single day in my life.'

_____

_____

c. 'And then a complete stranger kissed me on both
cheeks.'

_____

_____

_____

d. 'He was lucky to escape alive.'

_____

_____

_____

e. 'I find it takes me about six weeks to learn a language.'

_____

_____

_____

6 Mrs Ford is talking to Mr Todd, who works for a finance company. She wants a loan. Write in the questions he asks her.

Mr Todd Come and sit down, Mrs Ford.
Mrs Ford Thank you.

Mr Todd (a) _____
Mrs Ford Two thousand five hundred pounds.

Mr Todd (b) _____
Mrs Ford I want to buy a car.
Mr Todd I see. Could you give me some personal

details? (c) _____
Mrs Ford I'm a computer operator.

Mr Todd (d) _____
Mrs Ford Twelve thousand pounds a year.

Mr Todd (e) _____
Mrs Ford Yes, I am. I've been married for six years.

Mr Todd (f) _____
Mrs Ford Yes, we have two children.
Mr Todd I see you live in a flat. Is it yours, or

(g) _____
Mrs Ford No, it's ours.

Mr Todd (h) _____
Mrs Ford We've lived there for three years.
Mr Todd Well, that seems fine. I don't think there'll

be any problems. (i) _____
Mrs Ford I'd like it immediately, if that's possible.
Mr Todd All right. Let's see what we can do.
Mrs Ford Thank you very much.

7 Report Mr Todd's questions.

a. First he asked her

_____

b. Then he wanted to know

_____

c. He needed to know

_____

d. She had to tell him

_____

e. Then he asked

_____

f. For some reason, he wanted to know

_____

g. He asked her

_____

h. He needed to know

_____

i. Finally he wondered

_____

8 Read this report of a conversation.

I had a row with my wife last night. We don't usually row about anything, but when we do, it's usually about money. It was all about the gas bill. You see, I thought she'd paid it, but when I got home there was a letter saying the gas would be cut off. She thought I'd paid it, so the bill had just been there for a month. I tried to explain that she usually pays the bills because I pay the rent, which is a lot, of course, but she just accused me of spending my money on things for me while she had to spend all her money on things for the house. Anyway, we sorted it out in the end. I paid it.

From this report, write the dialogue between the husband and wife.

_____

_____

_____

_____

_____

_____

_____

_____

_____

_____

9 Reasons for complaint

Look at the list of reasons for complaint and match them with the items below.

It's torn.	There's a bit missing.
It's scratched.	It's cracked.
It's shrunk.	It doesn't work.
There's a mark on it.	It's stuck.
It's run out.	It died.

a jumper _____   a radio _____

a tie _____   a record _____

a plate _____   a book _____

a jigsaw _____   the switch on
a machine _____

a gas
lighter _____   a goldfish _____

Write a short story in the past tenses, using the opening and closing sentences given.

A few weeks ago I was looking for something to buy

_____ as a birthday present. I was in a

_____ shop when I saw _____

_____

_____

_____

_____

_____

_____

It just goes to show that it is worth complaining if you happen to buy faulty goods in a shop.

10 Phrasal Verbs

Sometimes when you look up a word in the dictionary you don't understand the definition, so you have to read the example carefully. Here are the examples that the *Oxford Advanced Learner's Dictionary* gives for five phrasal verbs with **put**.

The fireman soon **put** the fire **out**.
Please **put** this call **through** to the manager.
Put your books/toys **away**.
Put the rent **up** by 50p (a week).
The mere smell of garlic **put** him **off** his supper.

Complete these sentences using one of the above phrasal verbs.

a. I'm sorry. I didn't realize I couldn't smoke here.

I _____

b. Why don't you buy your car now? They're going to

_____ soon.

c. Hello, operator. Could you _____ extension 301, please?

d. I'll dry the dishes if you _____. I don't know where they should go.

e. The violence in America _____ going there for my holiday.

Here are five examples with **get** from the dictionary.

The new manager is easy to **get on with**.
Fred didn't remarry. He never **got over** the shock of losing Jane.
The books are locked up and I can't **get at** them.
Don't let this cold weather **get** you **down**.
How's Jim **getting on** at school?

Complete these sentences using a phrasal verb with **get**.

f. I must put this vase in a place where the children

_____ .

g. I know I shouldn't let his comments _____ but I can't help feeling upset.

h. How are you _____ in your new job?

i. **A** How _____ with your flatmate?
B Not very well at all. He is a smoker, and I can't bear the smell.

j. Jim's only just beginning to _____ his disappointment.

Revision

1   In this story there is one word missing from each line. Mark where the word should go, and write the word in the right-hand column.

I'd like ⋀ help you, but I'm too busy. Sorry.   *to*

Last week I walking in the street when I met
Peter, an old   _____

friend. He looked miserable, so I asked the
matter was, and   _____

he told he was having problems finding
somewhere to live.   _____

'Where you looked?' I asked. 'Everywhere,' he replied. 'If you _____

aren't quick, you find the flat has already taken. I get the _____

newspaper and if there's somewhere interesting I to take the _____

morning off work to look at it. I've looking for six months _____

now. If I don't find somewhere soon, I go crazy. I saw a place _____

this morning.' 'Really?' I said. 'What was it?' 'Well, it was _____

very nice. Not as big yours, but it was too expensive for me.' _____

I told him I like to be able to help, but my flat is already too _____

small, and my wife and I are thinking moving. I suggested that _____

he put an advert in the paper. I have some friends did that _____

recently. 'You never know,' I said, 'you find just what you're _____

looking for.' 'That's a good idea,' he said, 'I do it tomorrow.' _____

He asked me I knew which paper my friends had advertised in. _____

'I don't know,' I said, 'but if I were you, I try the *Evening* _____

Standard. It sold all over London, and there's a special section _____

for people looking flats. It's not too expensive, either.' _____

I haven't seen Peter then. I hope he has found somewhere by now. _____

2   The words in brackets can be used to form words that fit into the following sentences.

Sorry. Eleven o'clock is an *inconvenient* time for me. (convenient)

a. It is more _____ to buy a big packet of cornflakes than a small one. (economy)

b. John Jameson is a famous _____ who stole five million pounds from a bank. (crime)

c. I'm quite an _____ person. I play a lot of sport and go running every day. (energy)

d. _____ your own business can cause a lot of financial worries. (manage)

e. Churchill was not only a famous _____ but also a respected _____. (politics; history)

f. The surgeons tried their best to save his life, but unfortunately the operation was _____. (success)

g. I understand _____ what you're saying. (perfect)

h. Jane's _____ as director came as no surprise. (appoint)

i. A holiday in America can be _____ cheap. (surprise)

j. The _____ of the Hollywood actor, Jimmy Halton, was announced last night. (die)

k. My colleagues are very pleasant, but the manager is a little _____. (friend)

l. I _____ this morning, and was late for work. (sleep)

m. There have been great _____ in medical care in the last twenty years. (improve)

n. _____ is one of my favourite activities. (cook)

o. Some people have a great fear of _____ by plane. (travel)

3   Reply to these questions in a natural way.
   A   How do you find your English lessons?
   You *I like them. They're useful and interesting.*

a. **A**   How long have you been at this school?
    You _____

b. **A**   What have you been doing since I last saw you?
    You _____

c. **A**   What's Peter like?
    You _____

d. **A**   How do you spend your free time?

You _____

e. **A**   If you had a year free, and enough money not to need to work, what would you do?

You _____

f. **A**   How's Anne?

You _____

g. **A**   What are you doing tonight?

You _____

h. **A**   What are today's news headlines?

You _____

i. **Either A**   What do you like about your job?

   You _____

   Or   A   What job would you like to do?

   You _____

j. **A**   How long are you thinking of studying English for?

You _____

4 Write an appropriate question.

   You *Where do you come from?*
   A   I come from Spain.

a. **You** _____
   A   Because I need it for my job.

b. **You** _____
   A   Three. English, French, and of course, Spanish.

c. **You** _____ America?
   A   Yes, I have. Just once.

d. **You** _____
   A   I love it. I think it's a very exciting country.

e. **You** _____
   A   I went there on business. I had to go to a conference in Chicago.

5 Put the verbs in brackets in the correct tenses.
   Yesterday I *went* (go) to the park.

2011 Mountain Bd.,
Asheville,
North Carolina
September 16

Dear Suzanna,
   Thank you for your letter which I (a) _____ (receive) last week. It was really good to hear from you. You said you (b) _____ (see) Angela recently, but you didn't say how she (c) _____ (be). Please let me know, and give her my regards.

I (d) _____ (be) in Carolina for six weeks, and I'm enjoying life here very much. I (e) _____ (work) very hard since I arrived, but the job is interesting and everyone is very kind to me. When I arrived in the States I (f) _____ (stay) a few days in New York, and there something awful happened. My wallet (g) _____ (steal). While I (h) _____ (look) in a shop window on Sixth Avenue, I felt my shoulder bag move. I looked down at it and I realized someone had opened it and taken my wallet. If I'd been more careful, it wouldn't have happened. I (i) _____ (not see) the person at all.

But I'm trying to forget all that. I (j) _____ (live) in a small hotel at the moment, but someone in the office has asked me to share his flat with him. He seems a really nice chap. His name is Bill, he's from Carolina, and he (k) _____ (live) on the sixth floor of a big block.

It's a bit untidy at the moment because it (l) _____ (decorate), but it'll be fine. We've arranged everything, and I (m) _____ (move) in next week. I'd love a holiday, because the job is really tiring, and I don't think it'll get any easier. Some friends of mine (n) _____ _____ (go) on holiday soon. If I (o) _____ _____ (not have to) work so hard, I (p) _____ _____ (go) with them, but it's impossible at the moment.

You said you (q) _____ (come) to see me this Christmas. I hope you haven't changed your mind. Let me know what date you (r) _____ _____ (think) of arriving. If you (s) _____ (come), I (t) _____ _____ (show) you around. There's an awful lot to see.
Write soon.
Love,
Steve.

6 How much progress do you think you have made studying this book?

A lot?
Quite a lot?
An average amount?
Not much?
Very little?

What do you like doing most and least in the language classroom?

Discussion
Listening to tapes
Grammar and exercises
Vocabulary
Reading
Writing
Pronunciation

In what areas do you need to improve most?

Speaking accurately.
Speaking and perhaps making some mistakes, but getting my message across to other people.
Understanding what people say — they speak so quickly.
Fast reading — I'm too slow.
Writing accurately in different styles.
Pronunciation — people often can't understand me.
Vocabulary — I'm often lost for words.

How do you intend to improve in these areas?

Take every opportunity to speak English.
Buy a grammar book and do lots of exercises.
Listen to tapes, the radio, films in English.

Read as much as possible.
Keep vocabulary records and try to add a certain number of words each day.

UNIT 1

Exercise 1

a. makes
b. she's making
c. Something's burning
d. I'm working . . . I'm saving up
e. smokes . . . he's trying
f. rises
g. learns . . . she's having

Exercise 2

Sample answers

a. He's a vegetarian, so he never eats meat.
b. I don't smoke cigarettes, but I sometimes have a cigar after supper.
c. We always go to Italy for our summer holidays because we have a villa there.
d. In winter we sometimes go skiing in France, or we sometimes stay at home. It depends.
e. We don't often have fish because it is difficult to buy fresh.

Exercise 3

a. No, they don't.
b. Yes, they do.
c. Yes, I am.
d. No, she doesn't.
e. No, it isn't.
f. No, it isn't.
g. Yes, I do.
h. No, it doesn't.

Exercise 4

a. What do you do?
b. How many hours a week do you work?
c. Where do you teach?
d. How much do you earn?
e. How often do you go abroad?
f. Do you often go out in the evenings?
g. What sort of films do you like?
h. Where are you going?

Exercise 5

Sample answers

a. Ed is a policeman in New York. He directs the traffic, helps people in the street and gives them information. He tries to stop crime and catch criminals. He wears a uniform.
   At the moment he's at home with his family. He's doing the washing up, and his wife is playing with their son. He's wearing a T-shirt.
b. Amy and Peter own a restaurant. They serve English and French food. In the morning they buy all the fresh food, and then work hard in the kitchen to prepare it. They work very long hours, and finish after midnight. At the moment they are on holiday. Amy is lying next to a swimming pool. She is reading a book. Peter is swimming with his daughter.
c. Noriko is a doctor in Tokyo. She examines people who are ill, and tries to find out what is the matter with them. She decides what medicine to give them, and when they can go home.
   At the moment she's shopping. She's looking at a dress, and thinking of buying it.

Exercise 6

Sample answers

a. A newsagent sells newspapers, sweets, cigarettes, and birthday cards.
b. You go to a DIY (do-it-yourself) shop if you want to do some decorating or building in your own house.
c. An off-licence sells alcohol to take away and drink at home.
d. You save money at a building society, or you borrow money to buy a house.
e. A garden centre sells everything you need for the garden.
f. A book shop sells books.
g. You go to a library to borrow books.
h. An estate agent advertises houses that are for sale.
i. A jeweller sells watches, rings, bracelets, etc.
j. A hardware shop sells things made of metal for the kitchen (saucepans, knives, and forks) and home (nails, hammers).
k. A chemist sells medicine, make-up for women, shaving cream for men etc., and films for cameras.

l. A freezer centre sells frozen food.
m. A sports shop sells everything you need for all kinds of sports.
n. A florist sells flowers.
o. You go to a travel agent to book a holiday or to make travel arrangements.

Exercise 7

/z/ lives drives earns goes comes does
/s/ works starts takes gets likes meets
/ɪz/ finishes

UNIT 2

Exercise 1

Sample answers

a. Would you like something to eat?
    Yes, please. I'd like a sandwich.
b. Would you like to play tennis?
    Yes, I'd love to.
c. Would you like an aspirin?
    Yes, I would.
d. Would you like to borrow a jumper?
    Yes, please.
e. Would you like to visit the cathedral?
    Yes, I'd love to.
f. Would you like a game of cards?
    Yes, I would.
g. Would you like to watch television?
    Yes, I would.

Exercise 2

a. 5   b. 6   c. 1   d. 2   e. 4   f. 3

Exercise 3

a. I like black coffee.
b. He speaks three languages.
c. Correct.
d. Restaurants stay open late in Spain.
e. Correct.
f. He has a flat near the centre.
g. What do you think of Shakespeare?
h. Correct.
i. He's cooking breakfast.
j. Correct.

Exercise 5

1 b +	5 b −	8 b −
2 c +	6 a +	9 a +
3 a −	7 c −	10 c +
4 c +		

Exercise 6

a chef   a spoon   to roast   an oven
                a frying-pan
a businessman a briefcase   to make a profit
                a factory   the Stock Market

a nurse   a bandage   to give an injection
                an X-ray   a thermometer
an editor   an article   a headline   to interview
                a national daily paper

Exercise 7

a. I can see
b. He's listening to music
c. I like looking at
d. I usually watch
e. I can hear
f. I can't hear
g. Look at
h. Please listen to what
i. She's looking at
j. I can't see

UNIT 3

Exercise 1

a. I went
b. I decided
c. it was raining   I stepped   The sun was shining
    a cool wind was blowing
d. I took   I was signing   someone tapped   I turned
    He was staying
e. we went   street traders were selling   tourists were
    trying   we listened

Exercise 2

a. No, she didn't. She celebrated her 103rd birthday.
b. Yes, she did. Forty people came to her house.
c. No, she wasn't. She was born in Ireland.
d. Yes, she did. She went to London.
e. No, she wasn't. She was working as an air raid warden.

Exercise 3

a. How many schools did you go to?
b. What sort of schools were they?
c. Did you like your schools?
d. What exams did you take?
e. Did you go to university?
f. What did you study?
g. How long were you at university?
h. When did you leave?

Exercise 4

a. in the morning . . . at night
b. at weekends.
c. on Sunday morning . . . in the evening
d. in summer . . . at nine o'clock
e. in June . . . at Christmas
f. at 9.30 . . . on Fridays . . . at 8.30
g. in 1951

h. on 18 January, 1954.
i. on Christmas Day
j. in the nineteenth century

in the morning
   the afternoon
   the evening
   spring/summer/autumn/winter
   1985
   the nineteenth century

at night
   8.00
   Christmas/Easter
   week-ends

on Sunday morning
   Mondays
   Fridays
   Christmas Day
   my birthday

Exercise 5

/d/ rescued climbed arrived moved used stayed
/t/ hoped washed stopped walked helped crashed
/ɪd/ decided planted posted ended

Exercise 6

climb	know	sign	listen	island
theatre	talk	honest	cupboard	daughter
farm	comb	wrap	sandwich	calm
turn	autumn	write	centre	psychology
Wednesday	February	Christmas	iron	handkerchief

Exercise 7

a. birth
b. birthday
c. born
d. birth
e. born
f. died
g. death
h. dead
i. die
j. dead . . . die
k. married
l. married
m. get married
n. married
o. marry
p. got married
q. got married

Exercise 8

They were away longer than a fortnight.
He said they didn't go to any big towns, but then he said the children liked Paris.
He said they drove straight to the farm house, but then he said they stayed in a hotel.
He said they were renting the farm house, but then he said they were going to sell it.
He said they didn't have very good weather, but he also said they went swimming every day.
He said he bought some pottery for his father, but then he said he didn't buy any presents.
He said they didn't travel around, but then he said they bought some wine from a farm 60 kilometres away.

UNIT 4

Exercise 1

Sample answers
a. Could you give me the bill, please?
   Certainly, sir.
b. Shall I look at it for you?
   Oh, yes please. That's very kind of you.
c. I'll give you a lift, if you like.
   Thank you very much.
d. Could you give me a light, please?
   Yes, here you are.
e. Excuse me! Could you change a pound for me?
   Sorry, I can't.
f. I'll baby-sit for you.
   Oh, will you? That's lovely.
g. Could you turn your television down, please?
   Sorry. Yes, of course.

Exercise 2

Dialogue 1   k e g a j m f
Dialogue 2   c h l d n b i

Exercise 3

Sample answers
a. Could you take me to the airport, please?
b. Could you mend my washing machine, please?
c. Could you mend the lights in my house, please?
d. Could you get this stain out of my trousers, please?
e. Could you bring me breakfast in my room, please?

Exercise 4

a. Could you take
b. I've brought
c. Could you fetch
d. you should take
e. remember to bring
f. I've taken (or) I took
g. Could you fetch
h. Could you take
i. Could you fetch
j. bring it back

Exercise 6

a. ago
b. for
c. During
d. for
e. ago
f. for
g. ago
h. while
i. during

UNIT 5

Exercise 1

a. I'll send her some flowers.
b. I'll turn on the heater.
c. We're going to get married next year.
d. I'll help you.
e. I'll do it now.
f. I'll buy him a card.
g. I'm going to retire next year.
h. I'm going to cook for ten people.

i. I'll ring him and apologize.
j. I'm going to do it very carefully.

Exercise 2

Sample answers

a. I'll lend you some.
b. I'll send them a card.
c. I'll look it up for you.
d. I'll help you look for him.
e. I'll look in the paper.

Exercise 5

a. anything . . . any
b. something . . . some . . . anything
c. anyone . . . someone
d. some . . . some . . . any . . . any
e. some (or) any . . . somewhere

Exercise 6

a. extremely
b. unpleasant
c. inefficient
d. carelessly
e. unkind
f. unattractive
g. happily
h. unreliable
i. faultless
j. dangerously

Exercise 7

a. When you **grill** something, the heat is directly above
    or below the food.
    You **roast** something in oil in the oven.
    You **fry** something in oil in a frying pan.
    You **bake** something in the oven without oil.
    You **boil** something in water on top of the cooker.
b. Eggs.
c. **Cut** is the general word.
    Chop means to cut into small pieces.
    Peel means take the skin off, for example potatoes or
    apples.
d. **sweet** wine   a **rare** steak
    tender meat   a **thick** soup
    raw fish   a **light** meal
    stale bread   **overcooked** vegetables

Answers to the revision test

Question 1

a. arrived
b. ago
c. I'm staying
d. Mrs Bolton works
e. Mr Bolton doesn't have
f. He's going to do
g. I'm having
h. but
i. I would
j. interesting
k. I'll
l. I was travelling
m. when
n. we last saw
o. he was working
p. he's learning
q. We're going to see
r. I think
s. Could you
t. I'll pay

Question 3

Sample answers

a. I'm terribly sorry. I'll get a cloth.
b. Would you like to come to the cinema with me
    tonight?
c. Excuse me! Could you tell me how to get to the post
    office?
d. I'm sorry. I'm a stranger here, too.
e. I think you've made a mistake. I gave you a five
    pound note.

Question 4

Sample answers

a. because I didn't have a job.
b. so I looked in the newspaper.
c. but I soon got very depressed.
d. while I was looking in the window of a job agency
e. who wanted some help in his business, so I rang and
    got an interview.
f. they offered me the job.
g. the job isn't very interesting.
h. there are so few other jobs, so I'll have to stay.

UNIT 6

Exercise 1

a. What does she look like?
b. How is Alice?
c. What's she like?
d. Is there any food that you don't like?
e. What did the men look like?
f. How is your girlfriend?
g. What are the Bahamas like?

Exercise 2

Sample answers

a. I like reading, gardening, and all sport.
b. They're fine.
c. I look like my mother. We both have curly brown hair.

d. I'm a bit moody sometimes, but I try to be sincere and kind to other people.
e. It's very good. The building is modern, and the teachers are good. It's a bit expensive, though.
f. She's quite tall, with short black hair.

Exercise 3

Sample answers

Paul I've got a bit of a problem. I haven't got anywhere to live, and it's very difficult to find somewhere.

Paul Yes, I am.

Jeremy It's in West London, not far from a park, but it's on a main road next to a cinema. I suppose it could be a little noisy. It's got one bedroom, but it's quite big. There's a small living-room with a kitchen off it. The bathroom's very small, but it does have a garden.

Jeremy His name's Bill. He's Canadian, he comes from Montreal. He has a wife and two children, and they're super. Bill's a doctor and works at a local hospital. He's very nice. He likes going to the cinema and playing rugby. Oh, and he hates people who smoke.

Paul I can't tonight. I have to work. Do you think he'll be in tomorrow?

Jeremy Take the tube to Camden Town, turn left outside the station and take the first right. It's Lower Road, I think. Go up Lower Road and take the second on the left, and that's called Kingly Street. Then take the first on the right until you get to Princes Road and it's on the corner.

Exercise 4

a. blond hair/fair hair
b. a light room/bright room
c. a married person
d. a return ticket
e. a sour apple
f. dry wine
g. a weak man
h. mild beer
i. simple food/plain food
j. a poor person
k. an easy exam
l. a soft chair
m. a cold drink/a cool drink
n. a mild curry

Exercise 5

a. a wealthy man
b. a sad situation/a depressing situation
c. my normal routine
d. an amusing story
e. a smart person
f. a quiet voice/a gentle voice
g. a messy room
h. a naughty child

Exercise 6

Sample answers

a. France is bigger than England in area, but England has a bigger population.
b. My new job is very interesting. I have to work a lot harder than in my old job, and the hours are longer, but the salary is higher, so I don't mind. Also there are better chances of promotion.

c. I sold my Mercedes and bought a Mini because the Mini is much more economical. It's cheaper to run, and uses much less petrol.

UNIT 7

Exercise 1

a. came . . . arrived . . . went . . . has been
b. Have you seen her? . . . saw . . . Have you looked . . . went . . . asked
c. borrowed . . . I've lost . . . Where did you go? . . . What time did it happen? . . . left . . . chained . . . phoned . . . happened

Exercise 2

a. for
b. for
c. since
d. since
e. for
f. since
g. for
h. since
i. since

Exercise 3

a. What sort of car is it?
b. How old is it?
c. What colour is it?
d. How many owners has it had?
e. What sort of condition is it in?
f. How many miles has it done?
g. Have you had any accidents?
h. How much is it?

Exercise 4

What sort of car is it?
How long have you had it?
How much did you pay for it?
How many miles has it done?
When did you pass your test?
Have you ever had an accident?

Exercise 6

a 3   b 5   c 4   d 2   e 1

Exercise 7

a. we'll have to economize
b. its own economic problems
c. an economics lecturer
d. The most economical way
e. responsible for the economy
f. professional economists
g. The world economic situation
h. more economical
i. professional and business-like
j. shall we get down to business
k. Mind your own business (or) That's no business of yours. (The first is better.)

l. thinking of going into the textile business
m. go abroad on business
n. a receptionist's business to help clients and tell them which room they are in.

UNIT 8

Exercise 1

a. you should get
b. You shouldn't play
c. I had to call
d. I mustn't/shouldn't eat
e. I don't have to get up
f. You should keep
   I have to pay
g. I must remember
h. No one likes having to work
i. You don't have to come
j. I have to look
k. we had to wear
l. You mustn't touch
m. She has never had to do

Exercise 2

Sample answers

Obviously it is impossible to give absolute answers to these questions. It depends how well you know the people.

1 (a) or (b). Young people tend to take wine because it is quite expensive in England. Naturally it is polite to take some kind of gift, and flowers or chocolates are usually a good choice.

2 (a) or (c). (c) is probably the best, but if there are not many people, and your host hasn't introduced you, you could naturally do it yourself.

3 (a) or (b). It depends how well you know the people.

4 (a) or (c). There are no rules here. It depends on you. (b) is impolite.

5 (a) is very formal. (c) is possible but by no means obligatory. (b) and (d) are both possible — it depends on you.

Exercise 4

a. I
b. does
c. told
d. yesterday
e. after

Exercise 5

1 e	2 b	3 k	4 d	5 a
6 f	7 h	8 j	9 g	10 c
11 i				

Exercise 6

a. A surgeon performs operations.
b. A sister is a senior nurse in a hospital.
c. A consultant is an expert on a subject who can give specialist advice.

d. A midwife helps a woman in childbirth.
e. A dentist looks after your teeth.

UNIT 9

Exercise 1

a. you go
b. my wife was . . . I'd leave
c. it rains . . . we won't be able to play
d. I see . . . I'll tell
e. I don't like meat if it is undercooked.
f. you don't have . . . it'll go
g. I had . . . I'd take up
h. he was . . . he could be

Exercise 2

Sample answers

a. if your shoes need repairing.
b. you've hurt yourself.
c. you want to get married.
d. you want to bet on a horse.
e. you want a Chinese meal to eat at home.

Exercise 3

a 3   b 5   c 1   d 4   e 2

Exercise 4

make a mistake	make a will
make progress	make friends with
do someone a favour	do business with
make a speech	make a noise
do my homework	make a phone call
do his best	make sure that
make money	do an exam

make a complaint
make up my mind to
do nothing
make sense
make a mess
do the housework

a. Could you do me a favour?
b. I'm beginning to make progress.
c. I think you've made a mistake.
d. I do a lot of business with the Chinese.
e. They don't make sense to me.
f. I have finally made up my mind to accept the job.
g. Don't make a noise.
h. I'd like to make a complaint.
i. you should make sure that
j. I'm doing my best.
k. the Prime Minister made a speech
l. If you make a mess again,
m. I need to make a phone call.

UNIT 10

Exercise 1

a. you can get married
b. Women couldn't vote
c. I couldn't get
d. I thought I could smell gas
e. Could I make an appointment
f. I want to be able to service
g. animals can't see very well
h. you can do (or) you've been able to do

Exercise 2

Sample answers

a. Could I sit down here? (or) Is this seat free?
b. Would you mind if I made a quick call?
c. I'm awfully sorry. Can I pay you tomorrow?
d. Could I borrow a pen, please?

Exercise 3

Dialogue 1   j b e d k m h
Dialogue 2   n i a c g l f

Exercise 5

3 I did well at maths.
5 I was hopeless at maths.
2 I was very good at maths.
6 I knew absolutely nothing about maths.
1 I was best at maths.
4 I was quite good at maths.

3 I liked maths.
5 I disliked maths.
6/7 I hated maths.
2 I loved maths.
4 I didn't mind maths.
6/7 I couldn't stand maths.
1 Maths was my favourite subject.

Answers to the revision test

Question 1

a. has had	h. since	o. can't
b. for	i. has	p. like
c. most	j. should/will	q. would
d. became	k. has ruled	r. wasn't
e. until	l. does	s. would
f. could	m. will	t. would/will
g. has been	n. have read	

Question 2

Sample answers

Peter Fifteen new students have enrolled for next month, and a group from France have asked for special classes. I think we are going to need two more teachers.

Chrissy Why don't we put an advertisement in the paper?
Chrissy She's very reliable and hard-working. She's very friendly, and gets on well with people. And she's an experienced teacher; she's taught for six years.
Chrissy In Egypt and Spain. She's done special courses for business people in Sweden, and in fact has written a book. She trained with me in 1978.
Chrissy She's average height, dark brown hair, very curly. She's quite slim, and wears casual clothes. She's got a Scottish accent, and she's always laughing.
Chrissy If I see her tonight, I'll tell her about the job.

UNIT 11

Exercise 1

a. I've been working . . . I haven't finished yet
b. I've visited
c. Someone has taken . . . I've been looking
d. I've been shopping . . . I haven't bought
e. I have ever read
f. What have you been doing?
   I've been working in the garden . . . I've planted
g. I've been waiting . . . nobody has arrived

Exercise 2

a. It's raining . . . I haven't brought
b. uncle knows . . . He's been growing . . . he's trying
c. I've been listening . . . I haven't understood
d. I've been reading . . . I have (or) I've got

Exercise 3

Sample answers

a. They've been decorating downstairs.
   They've been arranging the furniture.
b. He's been working overtime.
   He's been putting half his salary in the bank.
c. I've been doing a lot of exercise.
   I've been eating a lot of fruit.

Exercise 4

Sample answers

a. He's been running upstairs.
b. He's been cutting the grass.
c. I've been polishing it.
d. It's been raining a lot.
e. I haven't been eating properly.
f. I've been burning leaves.
g. I've been mending a vase.

Exercise 5

company **that** produces
it **has** been
years. **Its** offices
It **employs** twenty-five
staff **of** five
been **working** for
has **been** using
its **goods.** It
several **times** to

Exercise 7

tea cup	writing paper
egg cup	wrapping paper
reading glasses	hot water bottle
sun glasses	medicine bottle
recipe book	washing machine
telephone book	sewing machine
Christmas card	football boots
birthday card	wellington boots

UNIT 12

Exercise 1

Sample answers

a. **A** Would you like a game of tennis on Monday
   afternoon?
   K Sorry, I'm going shopping.
b. **A** Why don't we go to the theatre in the evening?
   K It's a nice idea, but I'm having some guests for
   dinner.
c. **A** Kate, come shopping with me on Tuesday
   morning.
   K I'm afraid I can't. I'm going to the travel agent to
   book my tickets.
d. **A** Let's go out for a meal in the evening.
   K That's very kind, but I'm going to the cinema.
e. **A** Come for a drive with me on Wednesday morning.
   K I can't, I'm afraid. The plumber's coming to fix
   my washing machine.
f. **A** Would you like to come round for tea in the
   afternoon?
   K That's very kind, but I'm going to Anna's house.
g. **A** Let's have lunch on Thursday.
   K Sorry, I'm flying to Italy.

Exercise 2

Sample answers

a. **A** Do you think you'll pass your exam?
   B I might, but I doubt it. I haven't done much
   revision.
b. **A** Do you think Peter will get the promotion he
   wants?
   B Yes, I think he probably will. He's certainly the
   best man for the job.

c. **A** Do you think there'll be a nuclear war?
   B Well, there might, but I doubt it. I don't think our
   leaders are that stupid.
d. **A** Do you think we'll find a cure for cancer?
   B Yes, I think we will. An awful lot of research has
   been done.

Exercise 3

Sample answers

a. **A** How do you think you'll find the money to buy a
   car?
   B I might get a bank loan. It depends how much the
   monthly repayments would be.
b. **A** When do you think your book will be ready for
   publication?
   B It might be ready in six months' time. I haven't
   been doing much recently.
c. **A** Who do you think will get the job of Director?
   B Henry might. He's certainly got the right
   experience and qualifications.
d. **A** How long do you think your trip around the world
   will take you?
   B It might take a couple of years. It depends how
   long we stop in each place.

Exercise 5

a. Baby-sitters are people who look after children while
   the parents go out.
b. I'll look it up in the dictionary.
c. I'm looking for my glasses.
d. Look out!
e. I've been looking forward to meeting you for a long
   time.

Exercise 6

a. It is difficult to put out electrical fires.
   It is difficult to put them out.
b. I don't know how you can put up with so much noise.
   I don't know how you can put up with it.
c. Please put the books back on the shelves.
   Please put them back on the shelves.
d. We have put the meeting off until next week.
   We have put it off until next week.
e. Could you please put away all your clothes?
   Could you please put them away?

Exercise 7

a.	a cat	j.	a whale
b.	a bird	k.	a horse
c.	a bull	l.	a bear
d.	a lion	m.	a cat
e.	a mule/donkey	n.	a dog
f.	a fish	o.	a lion
g.	a parrot	p.	a snake
h.	a dove		
i.	a snake		

UNIT 13

Exercise 1

a. The letters are delivered at 8.00.
b. This hotel was built two years ago.
c. A lot of preservatives are used in food these days.
d. Has your question been answered?
e. Your keys were found on top of the photocopier.
f. Reference books should not be taken out of the library.
g. The rate of taxation has been increased to forty per cent.
h. Penicillin was discovered in 1928.

Exercise 2

a. the police have arrested
b. who robbed
c. money was stolen?
d. it was never found
e. Bloggs was sent
f. he escaped
g. he was arrested
h. he has been living
i. who arrested
j. he was caught
k. detective was watching
l. he could be sent
m. he would be imprisoned

Exercise 3

1 c	2 g	3 f	4 k	5 a	6 e
7 j	8 l	9 i	10 d	11 b	12 h

UNIT 14

Exercise 1

a. She said she was going to Paris.
b. The teacher told the students that it was time to start revising for the exam.
c. I thought the film would be interesting.
d. She said she couldn't help me because she had too much to do.
e. I was told that Ann had bought the tickets.
f. He told me that it had taken him three hours to get here because the roads were flooded.
g. She said she thought it was a crazy idea, and it wouldn't work.
h. The receptionist explained that breakfast was served between 7.00 and 9.00.

Exercise 2

a. talked
b. told
c. said/replied
d. explained
e. tell
f. speak
g. said/replied
h. tell
i. speak
j. said
k. speak
l. said

Exercise 4

a. He asked me where I was going.
b. She asked him if he wanted to go out for a meal.
c. They wondered why their guest was late.
d. She asked me if she could use my phone to make a local call.
e. The customs officer asked me which countries I had been to.
f. He asked me if I knew where Angela was living.
g. She asked them what colour they were going to paint the living room.
h. I wondered why she didn't talk to me any more.

Exercise 5

Sample answers

a. I wonder how many husbands she has had.
   I wonder what happened to them all.
   I'd love to know who she is.
b. I wonder where his money comes from.
   I wonder what he does all day.
c. I wonder why he kissed her.
   I wonder where they were.
d. I'd love to know what had happened to him.
   I wonder if he's injured.
e. I'd love to ask him how he does it.
   I wonder how he learns them so quickly.

Exercise 6

a. How much would you like to borrow?
b. What do you want it for?
c. What's your job?
d. How much do you earn a year?
e. Are you married?
f. Do you have any children?
g. do you rent it?
h. How long have you lived there?
i. When would you like to have the money?

Exercise 7

a. First he asked her how much she would like to borrow.
b. Then he wanted to know what she wanted it for.
c. He needed to know what her job was.
d. She had to tell him how much she earned a year.
e. Then he asked if she was married.
f. For some reason, he wanted to know if she had any children.
g. He asked her if she rented her flat.
h. He needed to know how long she had lived there.
i. Finally he wondered when she would like to have the money.

Exercise 9

a jumper — It's shrunk.
a tie — There's a mark on it.
a plate — It's cracked.
a jigsaw — There's a bit missing.

a gas lighter — It's run out.
a radio — It doesn't work.
a record — It's scratched.
a book — It's torn.
the switch on a machine — It's stuck.
a goldfish — It died.

Exercise 10

a. I'll put my cigarette out.
b. They're going to put up the price soon.
c. Could you put me through to extension 301, please?
d. I'll dry the dishes if you put them away.
e. The violence in America has put me off going there for my holiday.
f. where the children can't get at it.
g. I shouldn't let his comments get me down
h. How are you getting on in your new job?
i. How do you get on with your new flat-mate?
or How are you getting on with your new flat-mate?
j. beginning to get over his disappointment.

Answers to the revision test

Question 1

a. I **was** walking
b. asked **what** the
c. told **me** he
d. Where **have** you
e. already **been** taken.
f. I **have** to
g. I've **been** looking
h. **I'll** go
i. it **like**?' 'Well
j. big **as** yours

k. I **would** like
l. thinking **of** moving
m. friends **who** did
n. you **might** find
o. **I'll** do
p. me **if** I
q. **I'd** try
r. It **is** sold
s. looking **for** flats.
t. Peter **since** then.

Question 2

a. economical
b. criminal
c. energetic
d. Managing
e. politician . . .
   historian
f. unsuccessful
g. perfectly

h. appointment
i. surprisingly
j. death
k. unfriendly
l. overslept
m. improvements
n. Cooking
o. travelling

Questions 3

Sample answers

a. I've been here for three months.
b. I've been very busy at work.
c. He's quite tall, with short black hair. He's very friendly, always smiling.
d. I like gardening and reading.
e. I'd travel round the world in a yacht.
f. She's fine.

g. I'm going out to a restaurant.
h. Unemployment has dropped.
   There's been a bad rail crash in Manchester.
i. It's very interesting. My colleagues are very nice.
   I'd like to be an engineer.
j. I think I shall study it for nine months.

Question 4

a. Why are you learning English?
b. How many languages do you speak?
c. Have you (ever) been to America?
d. What did you think of it?
e. What were you doing there?
   (Why did you go there?)

Question 5

a. I received
b. you had seen
c. she was
d. I have been
e. I've been working
f. I stayed
g. my wallet was stolen
h. I was looking
i. I didn't see
j. I'm living
k. he lives
l. it is being decorated
m. I'm moving
n. some friends of mine are going
o. I didn't have to work
p. I would go
q. you were coming/you would come
r. you are thinking
s. you come
t. I'll show